T0345575

Seán Lemass

Seán Lemass

ROBERT J. SAVAGE

✳

Published on behalf of
the Historical Association of Ireland

UNIVERSITY COLLEGE DUBLIN PRESS
Preas Choláiste Ollscoile Bhaile Átha Cliath
2014

First published 2014 on behalf of the
Historical Association of Ireland by
University College Dublin Press

© Robert J. Savage, 2014

ISBN 978-1-906359-87-4
ISSN 2009-1397

University College Dublin Press
UCD Humanities Institute, Room H103, Belfield,
Dublin 2, Ireland
www.ucdpress.ie

*The right of Robert J. Savage to be identified as
the author of this work has been asserted by him*

Cataloguing in Publication data available from the British Library

Typeset in Scotland in Ehrhardt by Ryan Shiels
Text design by Lyn Davies
Printed in England on acid-free paper by
Antony Rowe, Chippenham, Wilts.

CONTENTS

This book is dedicated to my friend and brother Stephen

＊

FOREWORD

Originally conceived over a decade ago to place the lives of leading figures in Irish history against the background of new research on the problems and conditions of their times and modern assessments of their historical significance, the Historical Association of Ireland Life and Times series enjoyed remarkable popularity and success. A second series has now been planned in association with UCD Press in a new format and with fuller scholarly apparatus. Encouraged by the reception given to the earlier series, the volumes in the new series will be expressly designed to be of particular help to students preparing for the Leaving Certificate, for GCE Advanced Level and for undergraduate history courses as well as appealing to the happily insatiable appetite for new views of Irish history among the general public.

CIARAN BRADY
Historical Association of Ireland

PREFACE

This short study of Seán Lemass was first published in 1999 following the publication of John Horgan's 1998 landmark biography. Since that time a range of scholars have addressed the life and legacy of Lemass. These include biographies by Tom Garvin and Bryce Evans and a comprehensive collection of essays edited by Brian Girvin and Gary Murphy. All of these publications address the remarkable career of one of the most influential politician of twentieth century Ireland.

This study considers the evolution of Seán Lemass as a politician and statesman, exploring how he came to terms with a series of difficult challenges during his long political career. As Minister and Taoiseach Lemass was confronted by a series of crises that threatened to undermine the governments in which he served and the policies he wished to pursue. This book addresses how he responded to dire economic conditions, the thorny issue of Northern Ireland, and complex relations with both the British Government and the powerful Catholic Church. It also considers how Lemass introduced television, perhaps the most public and controversial symbol of change in Ireland during the 1960s. What emerges from this study is the portrait of a wily, determined and astute leader determined to move Ireland forward as a self-confident member of the European community.

ROBERT J. SAVAGE
October 2014

CHRONOLOGY OF LEMASS'S LIFE
AND TIMES

1899
Seán Lemass born in Dublin

1891
Death of Parnell

1912
Third home rule bill passed

1916
Easter Rising
Battle of the Somme

1920
Government of Ireland Act

1921
Anglo-Irish Treaty

1922
Irish Civil War

1926
Fianna Fáil established

1932
Fianna Fáil assumes power

1937
'De Valera's constitution'

1938
Anglo-Irish Agreement

1939–45
Ireland neutral during the Second World War, 'the Emergency'

1948
Coalition Government replaces Fianna Fáil

1951
Fianna Fáil returns to power

1954
2nd Coalition Government

1955
Ireland joins the United Nations

1956
IRA Begins the 'Border Campaign' lasts until 1962

1957
Fianna Fáil returns, will be in power for the next 16 years

1958
T. K. Whitaker produces the landmark 'Economic Development'

1959
Lemass becomes Taoiseach, Eamon de Valera elected president
Mise Éire made by George Morrison for Gael-Linn, with music by Seán Ó Riada

1961
Telefís Éireann launched

1962
Lemass makes formal application for entry to the EEC in Brussels

1963
British application to the EEC is rejected, Ireland defers its application.
Terence O'Neill succeeds Brookeborough as Prime Minister in Northern Ireland
President John Fitzgerald Kennedy visits Ireland

1965
Lemass meets O'Neill at Stormont, Anglo-Irish Free Trade Agreement

1966
Commemoration of 1916 Rising
Jack Lynch replaces Lemass as Taoiseach

1967
Foundation of Northern Ireland Civil Rights Association

1968
Northern Ireland Civil Rights Association organises March from Coalisland to Dungannon

1969
Northern Irish Prime Minister Terence O'Neill resigns
'Battle of the Bogside'

1970
Ian Paisley elected to Stormont and Westminster

1971
Seán Lemass dies 11 May

Introduction

Seán Lemass was born on 15 July 1899, in Ballybrack, County Dublin. He was the son of a hatter who conducted business in the heart of Capel Street, Dublin. The future Taoiseach's father, John Timothy Lemass, was a political activist and a supporter of the Irish Parliamentary Party; his grandfather was active in nationalist politics as a Parnellite. However, John's two sons, Seán and Noel, embraced the more 'advanced' form of nationalism espoused by Sinn Féin. Both joined the Irish Volunteers in January 1915 and participated in the 1916 Easter Rising.

Following his retirement from politics in 1969, Lemass offered some revealing autobiographical reflections in a series of interviews with Michael Mills of the *Irish Press*. While these interviews contain much valuable material, it is important to read Lemass's statements as those of a politician interested in presenting himself and his party as a positive force in post-independence Ireland. One of the more fascinating recollections describes how the youthful Seán and Noel Lemass were out for a walk in the Dublin hills on Easter Monday 1916 when they had a chance encounter with Eoin MacNeill, founder of the Irish Volunteers and ardent opponent of the rebellion. MacNeill was out cycling with his sons when he recognised the Lemass brothers and informed them of the events taking place in the city. Lemass recalled:

We were only young fellows, but, nevertheless, MacNeill got off his bicycle and . . . told us about the rising . . . He thought the rising was a big mistake and the end of everything he had been working for.'¹

Seán and Noel anxiously made their way to the city centre, hoping to contribute to the insurrection. As a 16-year-old, Seán Lemass found himself inside the General Post Office, armed with a shotgun, fighting alongside James Connolly, Patrick Pearse and Seán MacDermott.

Lemass survived the rebellion and was later involved in the War of Independence and the Civil War. John Horgan suggests that as a young volunteer Lemass was one of the notorious 'twelve apostles', a ruthless covert unit organised by the leader of the Irish Republican Brotherhood (IRB), Michael Collins. These men destroyed the British intelligence network in Ireland on 'Bloody Sunday', 21 November 1920, killing 14 members of the 'Cairo Gang', a crack unit of British intelligence agents handpicked by Winston Churchill to destroy Collins and the IRB. According to one of his contemporaries, during this period Lemass was fully involved in the 'armed struggle' and enjoyed, 'a great reputation as a very active street-fighter'.² In the aftermath of the 1921 Anglo-Irish Treaty, Lemass chose to stand with those who opposed the agreement as a betrayal of the revolution. In what became a tragic civil war, he joined Rory O'Connor, his commanding officer, Oscar Traynor and the senior surviving commander of the 1916 Rising, Eamon de Valera, in taking up arms against the newly formed Irish Free State.

Lemass played an active part in the event that eventually helped to precipitate the Civil War, as he was part of the anti-Treaty force that seized the Four Courts in Dublin in April 1922. He was taken prisoner when the newly formed Free State army captured the building. By the age of 22 Seán Lemass had survived battles at the General Post Office and the Four Courts, two engagements that were certainly definitive events in the turbulent period that witnessed the birth of the new Irish state. He escaped his captors after the fall of the Four Courts but was arrested again in November 1922 and was interned at the Curragh prison camp. Lemass remained a prisoner until his release in October 1923, when the body of his slain brother Noel was discovered in the Dublin mountains. Noel Lemass had been tortured before being shot twice in the head. His murder occurred at least four months after the ceasefire that ended the Civil War was declared. Although it was never proved, it is almost certain that Free State forces killed Noel Lemass. The murder convinced the future Taoiseach that political violence in Ireland had to be avoided at all costs. Seán Lemass certainly had reasons to be bitter towards his enemies, many of whom became his political opponents in the Dáil. Yet throughout his career he assiduously avoided addressing the subject of the Civil War for fear of dredging up what for many was a very painful past. He understood the anguish caused by the conflict, and in his first address to a Fianna Fáil Ard-Fheis as Taoiseach asserted: 'The old antagonisms have no place in the Ireland of tomorrow.'[3]

After the Civil War Lemass became increasingly unhappy with the policy of Sinn Féin, the anti-Treaty party that refused to recognise the legitimacy of the Irish Free State. He regarded the party as ineffective and believed it was held hostage to members he derided as 'cranks'.[4] Lemass argued that many republicans in the party did not have the vision to find a way out of the strait-jacket of non-recognition and abstentionism.[5] He supported de Valera's decision to endorse a new direction, one that argued that Sinn Féin should enter the Dáil once the hated oath of allegiance to the crown was removed. De Valera failed to convince Sinn Féin to accept this policy at a special Ard-Fheis in March 1926. This led de Valera to resign from the organisation and to consider leaving public life. According to de Valera it was Lemass who encouraged him not to give up and convinced him to form a new political party. Lemass pleaded with de Valera, 'We have to go on. We must form a new organisation along the lines you suggested at the Ard-Fheis. It is the only way forward.'[6] This new organisation, Fianna Fáil, was established in October 1926, and Lemass, as a founding member, demonstrated impressive organisational skills in helping mould the party into a powerful nation-wide organisation. By 1932 Fianna Fáil, under the leadership of de Valera, was strong enough to form a minority government with the help of the Labour Party. As one of de Valera's most trusted lieutenants, Lemass played an important role – along with Gerry Boland – in building the impressive political machine that until very recently dominated Irish political life. In 1932 Fianna Fáil began an unprecedented tenure in office that would last until 1948, when the first inter-party government displaced it. Under de Valera, Fianna Fáil formed two additional governments in the 1950s with 'the Chief ' remaining at the helm until he 'retired' to the presidency in 1959.

While de Valera was President of the Executive Council and later Taoiseach, Lemass held a number of critical posts in the cabinet. Initially he was Minister for Industry and Commerce, during the 'Emergency' he became Minister for Supplies, and he was named Tánaiste in 1945. During this period Lemass earned a well-deserved reputation for being an effective administrator. Throughout his ministerial career and his tenure as Taoiseach he promoted efficiency in all spheres of Irish life. Indeed, efficiency was Lemass's watchword: he encouraged it in the workplace, in government and in the classroom. For Lemass, efficiency was the most critical ingredient needed to transform Ireland into a modern, successful, European nation.

In 1959, at the age of sixty, Seán Lemass stepped out of de Valera's shadow to become Taoiseach. As leader, Lemass was to preside over a country undergoing tremendous social and economic change. In fact Lemass would prove to be a considerable agent in facilitating this transformation of Irish society. These efforts in particular will be the focus of the present study.

***

This short biography will explore why Seán Lemass has become such a critical figure in twentieth-century Irish history. As such, it will examine some of the pivotal issues that confronted Lemass during his career. Because Lemass was deeply involved in politics for more than 30 year before becoming Taoiseach the book will briefly examine his tenure as TD and minister in various Fianna Fáil governments. In 1959 Lemass emerged as a confident leader who had gained valuable experience in fighting political opponents both inside and outside Fianna Fáil. These battles would prove invaluable in helping Lemass to identify priorities, which in turn enabled him to harness the power of his office and lead Ireland out of the economic and social doldrums of the 1950s. Moreover, this book seeks to explain what differentiated Seán Lemass from his predecessors, especially from the towering figure of Eamon de Valera. In doing so, this volume will explore Lemass's legacy and consider how his policies helped to chart a new course for the Republic of Ireland. Lemass was Taoiseach during a period that many observers define as a 'watershed' in the history of modern Ireland. Although this view has become an oversimplification – and a cliché – it is difficult to deny that his economic and political initiatives were an important influence on events in Ireland long after he departed from the political stage. Seán Lemass is most closely associated with the remarkable transformation of Ireland's economy. Thus, this short biography will address his economic policies although it will also explore other political and social initiatives that influenced Lemass and set him apart from his predecessors. The following chapters will also consider how Lemass tried to engage the Catholic Church, the Unionist leadership in Northern Ireland and the British government and how he proved instrumental in deciding how television would be introduced to Irish society. By taking into account Lemass's policies, initiatives and programmes in these areas we will see how this quiet, un-assuming, yet tenacious politician helped reorient Irish politics during a 'watershed' period.

This book does not attempt to offer a comprehensive biography of Seán Lemass. Nor does it pretend to provide a concise political chronology of his career as politician or Taoiseach. John Horgan's admirable study, *Seán Lemass: The Enigmatic Patriot*, remains the authoritative biography although a number of more recent books and articles have contributed to a more comprehensive under-standing of his long political career. Horgan's book appeared after studies by Brian Farrell, Joe Lee, Paul Bew, Henry Patterson and Michael O'Sullivan began the process of addressing the Lemass legacy. Since then scholars have used a wide variety of sources to place the career of Lemass in a wider context. Brian Girvin and Gary Murphy produced a comprehensive edited volume, *The Lemass Era: Politics and Society in the Ireland of Seán Lemass* that was published in 2005. This study includes essays that explored a wide variety of subjects that helped define the Lemass era. Chapters by the editors along with articles from a range of scholars including Niamh Puirséil, Enda Delaney, Peter Murray, Maurice FitzGerald, Michael Kennedy, John Walsh, Roddy Flynn and this writer consider subjects including emigration, economics, cross border co-operation, education, film policy and Lemass's often difficult relationship with the media. Tom Garvin's 2009 book, *Judging Lemass: The Measure of the Man*, added another voice to those who have considered the impact of Lemass on Irish society.

His beautifully illustrated study supports a consensus that often presents Lemass as a maverick, a Taoiseach responsible for overseeing policies that transformed Ireland in the 1960s. More recently Bryce Evans has written *Seán Lemass: Democratic Dictator*, a critical biography that challenges the notion of Lemass as Ireland's great moderniser. This book has helped provoke a debate that has forced a reconsideration of the Lemass legacy. Evans's iconoclastic consideration of Lemass challenges what he sees as a consensus that too easily portrayed Lemass as the heroic antithesis of Eamon de Valera. Evans may be right in arguing that Lemass has been too easily 'left off the hook' but to be fair many historians have recognised the mistakes and miscalculations Lemass made over a long political career. Nevertheless Evans's biography will provoke some to think they may have been too 'soft' on Lemass: it certainly illustrates that reappraising iconic figures such as Lemass is critical to understanding the complexities of the Irish past.[7]

Because of the limitations imposed by this type of short biography, some important subjects will not be addressed. These include Lemass's education policy, his relations with the trade union movement and with the media, as well as other issues including foreign policy and its impact on Irish neutrality. Many of these topics are addressed in the studies mentioned above. Instead five areas that helped define the Lemass era have been chosen: the economy, partition, television, and his relationship with the Catholic Church, and the British government.

Lemass deserves to be understood as one of the most important political figures in twentieth-century Ireland. He was first and foremost a successful politician, a man who understood that gaining and holding onto political power was the ultimate priority in his chosen profession. He has often been praised for his sense of the practical, for making decisions that were difficult yet progressive. This political pragmatism was one of his most important assets because it enabled many of his initiatives to become government policy. Lemass is remembered as an activist, a leader who was not afraid of taking chances to achieve results. However, he was often frustrated by the limitations imposed upon him by opponents both inside and outside government. Lemass was ambivalent about the compromises he made as a political leader, understanding that they sometimes curbed his own desire to introduce change in Ireland. During his career he learned that compromise was an essential, if unattractive, component of political life. Although uncomfortable with placing politics before principle, he learned that this was the price of power. The chapters that follow will examine this remarkable politician and consider his impact and contribution to Irish society.

CHAPTER I

Seán Lemass and the Politics of Economic Policy

Fianna Fáil formed its first government six years after the party was established. Under the leadership of Eamon de Valera, Fianna Fáil enjoyed electoral success for a number of reasons. It campaigned on a platform promising a comprehensive housing programme, economic selfsufficiency, an increase in the size of the dole and repudiation of debts owed to London. One reason for the party's success lay in its ability to attack Cumann na nGaedheal as an overly conservative party that had failed to reinvigorate the Irish economy.

Fianna Fáil gained crucial support in the south and west by appealing to small farmers, promising progressive land redistribution schemes. The party's radical agrarian programme contrasted sharply with the staid policies of Cumann na nGaedheal because Fianna Fáil embraced the small farmer as an integral part of an independent, self-sufficient Irish nation. The party promised to help these farmers become productive members of the agricultural community. Fianna Fáil supported farms engaged in tillage and the production of grains for the domestic market, not the large-scale cattle ranching and dairying associated with Cumann na nGaedheal. The objective was establishing self-sufficiency in a wide range of areas – including grain production. This approach dovetailed with the policy of autarchy advocated by Fianna Fáil.

Lemass paid lip-service to this central element of early Fianna Fáil economic policy, but was never fully convinced that the small farms of rural Ireland could be saved. However, he understood that electoral support from the rural areas was vital to the political life of Fianna Fáil. In spite of his reservations, party rhetoric continued to define the small farmer as the backbone of independent Ireland. As a pragmatic politician, Lemass understood that political power took precedence over his own opinion of the value of the party's agrarian policy.

Lemass believed that the small farm, cherished in the political culture of Fianna Fáil, was obsolete and not economically viable. Later in his career his reticence waned and he openly questioned the ability of these farms to adapt to modern methods. He attacked 'incompetent or lazy farmers' who had no right to 'allow land to go derelict or to be utilised below its reasonable productive capacity'.[1] His proposal – that the state should identify and consolidate small, inefficient farms – amounted to ideological heresy and shows to what extent his ideas clashed with those of de Valera and party stalwarts who celebrated the place of the small farmer in Irish society. Lemass had no time for romantic notions of cosy firesides and 'comely maidens'.[2] Instead he encouraged the development of modern, highly productive farms that would produce for the export market.

In fact the agrarian policies developed by the party under de Valera's leadership failed to save the small farmer he so fervently idealised. During the 1930s Fianna Fáil could not stem the tide of internal migration to the larger towns and cities or the more traumatic external emigration abroad. The depopulation of rural areas proved a stubborn problem for successive governments for much of the century. In the years preceding the Second World War it became clear that curbing the trend of those leaving rural areas was impossible. De Valera admitted that 'the flight from the land is a fact . . . it is difficult to see how people can be kept back on the farm'.[3] A sense of defeatism pervaded de Valera's acknowledgement of the impossibility of recapturing an idyllic past.

In contrast, Lemass saw rural depopulation as an unfortunate, but natural, development – the price that had to be paid for modernisation:

> There is no such thing as a flight from the land. It is a normal and healthy feature of a national economy based on agriculture that there is a steady flow of manpower from rural areas to employment in non-agricultural pursuits.[4]

Lemass acknowledged the need to support agricultural expansion and encourage the growth of agricultural exports. His promotion of large, efficient, modern farms contrasted sharply with de Valera's policy of nurturing the small family farm. The modern, efficient farms that Lemass advocated would accelerate the 'flight from the land' that so troubled de Valera.

However, Lemass's primary concern was industrial development. He was, after all, urban in his outlook and not enamoured with the rural ideal that has so often been attributed to de Valera. He understood that his Dublin background made many Fianna Fáil members suspicious of his policies and later in his career remarked that his urban background: 'had been advanced as an argument against . . . [my] becoming Prime Minister'.[5] As a young politician he was influenced by the economic philosophy of Sinn Féin articulated by Arthur Griffith, who maintained that Ireland would never be truly politically independent unless it first became economically independent. As early as 1929 Lemass proved his protectionist credentials by arguing against foreign investment.

He warned that Ireland's sovereignty could be compromised by foreign capital: 'Those who control industry can exercise a considerable influence on the determination of national policy ... They will undoubtedly render it difficult to adopt measures designed to protect national interests when those interests are in conflict with their own.'[6]

Accordingly, to win economic independence a protectionist policy was developed under Lemass's direction in his capacity as Minister for Industry and Commerce and put in place in the 1930s. This policy accepted basic Sinn Féin principles, which maintained that nascent Irish industries had to be shielded from foreign competition in order to prevent them from flooding the small Irish market with cheaply produced goods. Protecting the domestic market meant imposing tariffs on products that were manufactured abroad. Protection was intended to give native companies a chance to become competitive by providing an advantage in the home market over less expensive, mass-produced, foreign goods. The government hoped that sheltered industries would gain the critical experience needed to become efficient, and ultimately competitive, on the world market. This efficiency would lower production costs as well as costs to the consumer, making domestically produced goods attractive. At this point tariffs could be relaxed, as Irish products would be capable of competing against foreign-made goods. In such circumstances competitive native industries employing Irish citizens would thrive, creating jobs and increasing the standard of living. Lemass hoped that these policies would encourage the expansion of a strong working class as well as a more substantial middle class.

In 1932, when the first Fianna Fáil government came to power, Ireland found itself in the midst of a worldwide depression. Fianna Fáil also inherited a stagnant economy characterised by high levels of unemployment. Although emigration had slowed owing to the depressed US and British economies, it resumed later in the decade. The discouraging economic picture was quickly made more troublesome by the trade dispute known as the 'Economic War'. Upon taking office, de Valera suspended payment of annuities to the British Exchequer, arguing that the payments created an unfair burden to the fledgling Irish state. London retaliated by imposing tariffs on Irish exports, especially cattle.

As Minister for Industry and Commerce in this first Fianna Fáil government, Lemass was responsible for putting forward a strategy for industrial development. Although he declared himself a 'pragmatic protectionist', once in government events forced his hand.[7] With the Economic War in full swing, Lemass oversaw the passage of the Control of Manufactures Acts between 1932 and 1934. These measure encouraged Irish-owned companies to expand by limiting the ability of foreign firms to conduct business in Ireland. The legislation required new firms established in Ireland to be at least 50 per cent Irish owned. During this period Lemass oversaw the imposition of tariffs on a wide range of foreign-made goods.

In the first tumultuous Fianna Fáil government economic planning did not receive a high priority. Moreover, the trade war with Britain complicated Lemass's efforts to encourage industrial development. In these difficult circumstances, improvisation was critical and Lemass was forced to intervene directly in the economy. The 1937 Control of Prices Act proved that the government had to act to protect Irish consumers against high prices sought by protected Irish manufacturers. One historian points out that 'the writings of Arthur Griffith provided singularly sparse guidance on the actual mechanics of industrialization behind tariff walls.'[8]

At first the economic policies Lemass initiated showed some success inducing 'an initial spurt in manufacturing output and employment. Recorded output and employment rose by one-third within a few years '.[9] 'Industrial employment increased from 110,588 in 1931 to 166,513 in 1938, and industrial output increased by 40 per cent between 1931 and 1936.'[10] However, in spite of these achievements the economy remained deeply troubled. Throughout the 1930s the national income stagnated and unemployment remained high. This slowdown highlighted the fact that industrial expansion was limited to the domestic market. Trying to turn the economy around in such complicated circumstances, and in the midst of a worldwide depression, proved a difficult undertaking.

The Economic War ended when de Valera and the British Prime Minister, Neville Chamberlain, signed the 1938 Anglo–Irish Agreement. One year later, with the outbreak of the Second World War, the government faced what it termed 'The Emergency'. Confronted with shortages of vital supplies such as fuel and medicine, which threatened to cripple the economy, the Fianna Fáil government was forced to take extraordinary measures. While the war produced many challenges, it presented Lemass with a unique opportunity when de Valera named him the minister in charge of the newly created Department of Supplies.

Lemass quickly rose to the challenge, co-ordinating the allocation of precious wartime commodities that were critical for the survival of neutral Ireland. As the Second World War progressed, Lemass used his extraordinary ministerial powers to ensure that a basic standard of living was maintained. He became 'a kind of economic overlord charged with the vital responsibility of feeding, fuelling and clothing the nation'.[11] He established price and wage controls, which succeeded in keeping the economy from becoming completely dysfunctional by the pressure created during the war. Further, having such absolute power over the economy gave him the opportunity to appreciate the advantages of strategic planning.

Lemass's journey from protectionist to advocate of Keynesian economics has been well documented elsewhere.[12] It is clear that as

early as 1942 Lemass recognised the shortcomings of the protectionist policies he had helped put in place. In June of that year he
circulated to his cabinet colleagues a paper entitled simply 'Labour
Policy'.[13] In this document Lemass expressed concern about the
social and economic problems that he believed would challenge
post-war Ireland. He warned his colleagues that the return of
thousands of Irish workers from British factories at the end of the
war could create tremendous social and political problems for the
Irish government.

Lemass argued that it was imperative that steps be taken to
provide significant employment opportunities for the returning
emigrants. His call for the creation of a powerful Department of
Labour and a comprehensive programme of economic expansion
alarmed his fiscally conservative cabinet colleagues and failed to
gain the critical support such a venture required from the ever-
cautious Eamon de Valera.[14] Without the support of the Taoiseach,
Lemass's Labour Policy was side-lined by being passed on to a
committee, which ensured that the plan never got off the ground.
The Committee of Economic Planning that was established to
consider the proposals included de Valera, Lemass and his rival in
the cabinet, the Minister for Finance Seán MacEntee. It became
clear that Lemass had little support for the initiative; the committee
was unwilling to undertake the risks required by the ambitious
programme that he had presented. Cabinet colleagues were also
wary of the power Lemass amassed in his role as Minister for Supplies
and were loath to enhance his already considerable influence.

Lemass did not give up easily, however. A short time after his
1942 proposal had been thwarted he produced another memorandum that praised the general thrust and philosophy of Britain's
1944 white paper entitled 'Full Employment'. The comprehensive
memorandum has been described as proving Lemass's: 'full con-
version to Keynesianism.'[15] In this document he openly criticised

the attitude of the Department of Finance for failing to appreciate the need to encourage economic development. A short time later he produced another important memorandum advocating full employment. This proposal, according to one assessment, 'met with overwhelming opposition – not only from the majority of his cabinet colleagues and from the civil service, but from industrialists, bankers, and farmers, more concerned with rapid profit accumulation in the short term than with long-term planning.'[16]

In public Lemass did not present himself as having moved to the left of his colleagues in Fianna Fáil. The battles he fought were private ones waged quietly within the cabinet.[17] Although he disagreed with Fianna Fáil economic policy he remained a loyal party man and did not exploit the growing public discontent with the government's handling of the economy. Ever the pragmatic politician he: 'put the unity of his party before the necessity for radical economic change and dedicated himself in public to dampening down popular expectations and demands for innovation.'[18]

Lemass's efforts to encourage the cabinet to depart from fiscal orthodoxy were frustrated on a number of occasions over the next 15 years. His efforts to convince colleagues to take the initiative and actively engage in a sustained effort to rebuild the economy were thwarted. He was defeated by opponents in the cabinet, especially Minister for Finance Seán MacEntee, whose opposition to Lemass's initiatives lasted well into the 1950s. Historian Ronan Fanning has chronicled the struggle between Lemass and Finance in his exhaustive study, *The Irish Department of Finance 1922–1958*, at every juncture the powerful Department of Finance, with the support of the cautious de Valera, frustrated Lemass's efforts.

Lemass's advocacy of guarded Keynesian economics illustrates that he understood that the conservative fiscal policies that Finance embraced – and the government supported – had failed. His desire to shift Fianna Fáil economic policy met with stiff resistance from entrenched interests inside the party. By the spring of 1945 the entire cabinet was absorbed into the Committee of Economic Planning, and the initiatives Lemass developed had been effectively buried. In that same year de Valera appointed Lemass as his Tánaiste. However, this new position did not help him convince his colleagues to accept his arguments.

Lemass had put Ireland's protectionist policies in place in the 1930s, during the trade dispute with London. In fact the Economic War provided cover for Fianna Fáil as it propagandised that the suffering caused by the economic dispute was part of a larger patriotic struggle against Ireland's colossal neighbour. Under de Valera, protectionism was converted from an economic policy to an ideological one. In this 'David versus Goliath' scenario, it made sense to use protectionism as a moral weapon to challenge perfidious Albion. However, Lemass saw things differently, and one observer has succinctly described the resulting tension:

> For de Valera protection was to some extent an end in itself. He believed that the material wants should be limited and that 'frugal comfort' should suffice for the good life. Lemass did not share that ideal. For him protection was merely a means to an end. That end was a competitive Irish industry, which would create enough jobs to end involuntary emigration, and duly lead to a reversal of the population decline that had, in his view undermined both the economy and the national morale since the Famine.[19]

By 1948 a stagnant post-war economy that had created high levels of unemployment, low wages and continued rationing helped defeat the Fianna Fáil government.[20] The first inter-party government – comprising Fine Gael, Labour and the new Clan na Poblachta – displaced de Valera's government, which had been in power for 16 years. This disparate coalition shared at least one passion, a loathing for de Valera and Fianna Fáil. While in opposition, Lemass was a consistent and often abrasive critic of the coalition government. He became managing director of the *Irish Press*, the newspaper representing Fianna Fáil interests, and challenged his opponents both in the paper's columns and from the opposition benches in the Dáil.

Lemass did not present himself as a full-fledged convert to Keynesian economics during this period. Although he illustrated sympathy for the philosophy espoused by John Maynard Keynes, he was not consistent in this regard. While in opposition, politics, not logic, dictated that he denounce policies pursued by the first Inter-Party government. For instance, in 1949, Lemass vehemently opposed the establishment of the Industrial Development Authority, an organisation intended to encourage and co-ordinate investment in Ireland. He was critical of the coalition government's efforts to encourage foreign investment, though he knew that foreign capital would be a critical component of the type of expansion that he advocated.

These contradictions illustrate an ambivalence in the thinking of Lemass and led the authors of one analysis of his career to argue that they prove a 'willingness to compromise with the conservative elements in the Fianna Fáil Party and the business community who opposed further state intervention in the economy'.[21] The contradictions can best be explained by considering the politics of the day both inside and outside Fianna Fáil. In spite of the obvious difference of opinion between Lemass and senior members of the party, it was important for party leaders to display a degree of solidarity when out of power. The presentation of a 'united front' on such an emotive issue as economic nationalism was a way to reassure an electorate that had rejected the 'republican party' in 1948. Lemass was first and foremost a pragmatic politician; he understood that regaining political power was imperative. For

Lemass, in this instance and in others, principle took a back seat to political power.

The 1950s proved to be perhaps the most difficult decade in the early life of independent Ireland. A stagnant economy, stubbornly high levels of unemployment and relentless emigration challenged both coalition and Fianna Fáil governments throughout the decade. When Fianna Fáil regained power in 1951, the party remained in a weak position owing to its minority status, as it was dependent on the support of independent deputies in the Dáil. The government was still committed to supporting the fiscal orthodoxy espoused by Seán MacEntee who remained Minister for Finance. Lemass once again found himself outside the party's inner circle: his ideas for dealing with the economic crisis that gripped the country were ignored. Economic historian Cormac Ó Grada points out that

> Real national income virtually stagnated between 1950 and 1958. The industrial sector continued to rely almost exclusively on a stagnant domestic market. Net agricultural output (including turf) rose by only 7 per cent between 1950–2 and 1958–60.[22]

During this dark decade a pervasive sense of despondency descended over the country.[23] But, while his initiatives languished, Lemass remained convinced that risks would have to be taken to revive the economy. He grew impatient with the inability of Irish trade unions, manufacturers, banks and farmers to make the adjustments necessary to stimulate the economy. He argued that an increase in agricultural and industrial production was critical to the nation's future economic health. Lemass knew that protection had not produced lean, efficient companies that were ready to take on international competition. He made it clear that he saw the policies of protection that he had himself done so much to promote in the 1930s as having served their purpose. Hence in 1952 Lemass placed the Federation of Irish Manufacturers on notice. Addressing the association, he warned of changes ahead, maintaining that high production costs for Irish manufacturers would not be tolerated:

> The case for protection policy was that, by assuring the available market to Irish industries, it created the opportunity of expanding output and thereby getting unit costs down. The danger of it was that it might come to be regarded, both by factory owners and their staffs, as an acceptance by the Irish community that the costs must necessarily be higher here then elsewhere and an assurance that higher prices would be permanently accepted.[24]

A short time later Lemass returned to the need to re-examine trade and tariff policies by announcing that new trade legislation would be introduced in the Dáil. Although the inter-party government had raised the issue of revising restrictive trade laws, it had failed to follow through on its plans. Lemass was aware that for decades the government had encouraged the development of virtual monopolies geared to the domestic market. Protecting industrialists from competition by using tariffs and discouraging foreign investment helped create factories that produced expensive, poorly made goods. Consumers complained about the price and quality of products manufactured behind the high tariff walls Lemass had erected. One Swedish banker inspected a number of new factories and commented: 'Few seemed . . . well run, many have been sited with no regard to cost.'[25]

Lemass understood the problems inherent in protecting the native market, and during the summer of 1952, he drafted legislation that established a board empowered to investigate and penalise companies found guilty of conducting unfair trade practices. In pushing this legislation the Tánaiste was under no illusion about the opposition that he would encounter. In October 1952 he received a deputation from the Association of Chambers of Commerce in Ireland which complained bitterly of the proposed legislation. The apprehensive industrialists asked that the bill be withdrawn, arguing that it was not in the public interest. They suggested that in its place a commission be established that would consider complaints from consumers as well as decide whether legislation was in fact needed. Lemass held firm, explaining to the delegation that 'there was no prospect of the Bill being withdrawn'.[26]

Later that month, in a speech to the Dublin Chamber of Commerce, Lemass exploited a report by an US firm hired to examine the Irish economy by the previous government. The report provided the ammunition Lemass needed to warn the Irish business community that he would not permit protection to stand in the way of economic development. He told the Chamber of Commerce that:

> All of these outside experts had commented on the prevalence in this country of restrictive practices of one kind or another which they said were hampering the expansion of economic activity. They had pointed out the folly of talking about expansion and practicing restriction. They said they found a disposition in favour of restrictive practices in every sector of our national life, in business management, in agriculture and in trade union policy.[27]

It is clear that Lemass accepted much of the critique that had been made in the U.S. report. His call for a 're-examination of policies and practices, in the interest of progress' created unease in business circles.[28] Although Lemass was not endorsing unrestricted free trade, he was warning that the tariffs and restrictions against foreign investment that had long protected native industry would be revised. Despite the fact that Lemass was arguing for fundamental changes in the handling of the economy, his arguments were continually ignored. Floating these ideas at a time when the economy was in recession, and when emigration and unemployment threatened the social cohesion of the country, had little impact.

The Fianna Fáil government of 1951–4 did not instil any sense of confidence during this time of crisis. The government appeared weak, confused and unsure of itself. When interviewed by Michael Mills in 1969, Lemass carefully admitted that this government was a failure:

> It was not our most successful period in office . . . We felt hamstrung by the insecure position in the Dáil and we had not really gotten down to clearing our minds on post-war development.[29]

The failure to have 'clear minds on post- war development' was due to the continued dominance of the Department of Finance and its minister, Seán MacEntee. In 1952 MacEntee introduced an infamous budget that sought to deal with the balance-of-payments crisis confronting the government. In this budget taxes were increased by a shilling in the pound and the prices of commodities such as: fuel, butter, tea, sugar and alcohol were raised. Launched in the midst of a recession, the budget only aggravated the crisis and created a surge in unemployment and emigration. At the time the deflationary budget represented a victory for MacEntee and his brand of economic orthodoxy over Lemass, who advocated applying limited Keynesian economic policies to the troubled Irish economy.

MacEntee's victory was short lived, however, since although his policies helped to relieve the balance-of-payments crisis, they ultimately punished ordinary consumers and voters - who, in turn, voiced their dissatisfaction with Fianna Fáil in the 1954 General Election. Thereafter a coalition government returned to power and John A. Costello once again became Taoiseach, heading an unstable government that eventually collapsed in March 1957. The second inter-party government also proved unable to turn around the moribund economy.

When Fianna Fáil returned to power in 1957, de Valera was at the helm, although Lemass, as Tánaiste wielded considerable power. Lemass gained new credibility after the disastrous deflationary policies pursued by the last Fianna Fáil government. In 1957 Lemass's bête noire, Seán MacEntee, who had been discredited by his performance in the early 1950s, was exiled to the Department of Health at Lemass's insistence. This move was an important change and was, in fact, the only really significant one that occurred: the cabinet assembled in 1957 closely resembled the cabinet of 1951–3.

Lemass was fully aware that the problems that confronted the new Fianna Fáil government were considerable; at a Fianna Fáil dinner he spoke of the stark challenges confronting the nation:

> It is not an exaggeration to say that the next five years will prove whether this state can survive as an independent economic unit. This is the critical phase of our national development. All the years of sacrifice and struggle of the past will be, in these years, either justified or proved fruitless. The question is whether our people – on the farms, in the factories, and in all other spheres of activity – will put into the campaign to expand the national resources, the very great and sustained effort which will save the country.[30]

In October 1955, Lemass made his now famous speech in the ballroom of Clery's Hotel, calling for the creation of 100,000 new jobs. The speech was a wake-up call for Fianna Fáil and explicitly challenged the party to accept that radical new policies would have to be developed to attack the economic ills that plagued the nation. The address, entitled 'Proposals for a Full Employment Policy', was 'designed by Lemass to cut through the complacency with which his party contemplated inevitable electoral victory and forced [it] to consider a new approach'.[31] The speech illustrates that any ambivalence that had characterised Lemass's thinking on the need to embrace Keynesian economics had vanished.

By 1958 a consensus had emerged, indicating that a new direction was needed to prevent catastrophe in Ireland, and Lemass stepped into the void left by the failed policies of MacEntee. His call for the expansion of the economy and for productive government investment gained a good deal of credence – especially with his old rival Seán MacEntee side-lined in favour of the less doctrinaire Minister for Finance, Dr Jim Ryan. Although not articulated in a comprehensive manner, a growing sense now pervaded that the government's economic policy had to be completely reoriented. The crisis that threatened the state meant that chances would have to be taken and that risk – the bogey of the mandarins of Finance – would have to be accepted as official government policy. It quickly became clear that the state would become active in trying to influence and encourage the growth of the economy. This meant that planning was key, and that the age-old economic policies were expendable.

As historian J. J. Lee has written, the stature of Lemass grew in the dark crisis years of 1955–7. The 1956 census, underlining the decline in the nation's population, sent a shudder through Irish society that reverberated deep into the apparatus of the state; the census was a shock 'that convinced some key figures, most notably in Finance of the necessity for a fundamental change in direction. It was the closest Irish equivalent to the shame of surrender and occupation for continental countries in the Second World War.'[32] Simply put, the country was in grave trouble. Emigration was bleeding the country: 'nearly 200,000 [emigrated] between 1951 and 1956, another 212,000 in 1956–61; by 1961 the population had fallen to 2.8 million, more than 5 per cent below the level at the foundation of the state.'[33]

It was a result of this crisis that 'Economic Development', perhaps the most important document written during the life of the Irish state was drafted. Its author, T. K. Whitaker, was a remarkable civil servant who had risen quickly through the ranks to become secretary of the powerful Department of Finance in 1956. Whitaker advocated the creation of a comprehensive five-year plan that would embrace an integrated approach to economic development. He argued in unambiguous terms that it was essential that a co-ordinated effort be undertaken by the government to address the crisis that threatened the viability of the state. Whitaker's report became the basis for the government's white paper entitled 'Programme for Economic Expansion', which was published in November 1958.

Lemass supported Whitaker in his call for a drastic overhaul of the economic policies that Fianna Fáil had endorsed since the party first came to power in 1932. Eamon de Valera, while receding into the background, supported the new programme. The document argued that the country needed to set a target of two per cent annual growth over five years and that the state should undertake as much productive investment as possible – that is, investment that would help encourage or facilitate economic expansion.

Before the publication of the white paper, Lemass had outlined the government's ideas, pointing out in simple terms the need for drastic action. In January 1957, while still in opposition, Lemass told his party's consultative council that,

> So long as there is freedom for families to move to Britain, our standards must approximate to British standards or our population

will go. It is the survival of the nation which is involved, and not
merely our living standards, unless we can achieve, by our own efforts,
a rapid and substantial increase in our resources.[34]

Lemass wanted the government to expand national production by
one eighth by making an investment of between £50 and £60
million. He warned the public that these funds would have to be
raised out of current income and called upon the employed public
to make a commitment to an additional five per cent in savings. He
cautioned that, unless these savings found their way into Irish
banks, and thus became the resources needed for investment, taxes
would have to be raised. According to his plan, if the government
succeeded in putting the economy on a 'sounder basis', then

> the country could be asked to take a chance on the future and to
> expand expenditure on capital account by Government agencies and
> public authorities to increase employment immediately, in advance of
> the increase in national resources. That may mean a further encroach-
> ment on external reserves, and it is quite a chance to take. It is a question
> of balancing risks. This country cannot afford to drive its people away
> by deliberately depressing trade and employment. Apart from the
> local loss of productive personnel, the effect on the national morale is
> critical. The restoration of the confidence in the country's future is an
> essential part of the whole campaign for economic recovery.[35]

Speaking at University College Dublin, just after the publication
of the white paper, Lemass explained the 'Programme for Economic
Expansion' and why the government chose to publish its plan:

> There has been some evidence in recent years that people were
> beginning to question whether really substantial economic progress
> was possible at all or even whether a viable economy could be sustained

here. These questions needed to be answered, our people's confidence in the country ' s future needed to be supported, and the interest and enthusiasm of young people in national development needed to be stimulated.[36]

Lemass argued that the publication of a comprehensive programme was needed, 'based on an objective appraisal of the country's potentialities and present deficiencies and a realistic, even conservative, assessment of its development possibilities'.[37]

The Tánaiste made it clear that the objective was to increase efficiency and productivity – with an eye to the export market. The government committed itself to encourage export-oriented businesses from abroad to establish operations in Ireland. Such businesses were offered substantial tax incentives to locate in Ireland. Lemass knew that these policies might antagonise powerful supporters of Fianna Fáil, especially those in the business community. However, it was understood that a new departure would have to be made; in the words of J. J. Lee:

> [Lemass] hoped that the foreign firms would offer a model to Irish management and also create the breathing space in which protection could be greatly reduced, Irish firms modernised through specific equipment grants, and a refurbished industrial base be created which would quickly allow Irish industry to achieve sustained export growth in its own right.[38]

Although never optimistic about the ability of Irish farmers to become more productive, Lemass argued that expanding agricultural production would accompany the industrial expansion: 'Meat-cattle and sheep, beef and mutton – seem to offer the best chance of expanding our exports.'[39]

To do this, new energy would be put into marketing, breeding, providing subsidies for fertiliser, and expanding credit and advisory facilities. Manufacturing would also receive the special attention of the government. Lemass noted that Ireland had been successful in expanding industrial development to meet domestic needs, and that the challenge in 1958 was to expand industrial output for the export market; new methods that the government would push:

> The urgency of industrial progress lies in the fact that it is mainly by increasing the number and variety of jobs in manufacturing industry, that the speedy curtailment of unemployment and emigration can be brought about.[40]

In June 1959, at the age of 60, Seán Lemass became Taoiseach. His elevation was expected and unopposed. One might argue that, at his age, he hardly represented a new generation of leadership. However, it is important to remember that Lemass was replacing an ageing de Valera, who 'retired' into the presidency at the age of 74. Many commentators have mentioned the fact that general turnover of personnel in Irish politics would follow the advent of Lemass. Both Labour and Fine Gael would thus see new leaders replace the older generation.

Lemass wasted no time in establishing his plan for economic development. He remained committed to transforming the Irish economy and looked to European engagement for a number of reasons. By 1958 he had come to accept that free trade was inevitable and began preparing Ireland for the day when all restrictive tariffs would become obsolete. In 1960, Ireland decided to join with many developed and underdeveloped nations that became party to the General Agreement on Tariffs and Trade (GATT). A year later the government applied to join the European Economic Community

(EEC), as Lemass believed that the EEC would help Ireland find new markets for agricultural and industrial goods. He was also looking for inward investment, hoping that Ireland could attract foreign capital. Lemass began dismantling the Control of Manufacturers Act in 1958; by 1964 the act had been all but nullified. In its absence, foreign investment increased dramatically.

Lemass looked to Europe, as he believed that prosperity for Ireland lay in becoming trade partners with European nations. He longed for the day when Ireland could join with the rest of Europe in a common market where the importance of borders would become less significant. He was disappointed that Ireland's application for membership of the EEC had to be set aside in 1963, after the rejection of Britain's application. However, he remained committed to preparing Ireland for eventual entry into Europe.

In the meantime Lemass worked toward establishing a new trade pact with Britain. He had begun the process of cutting tariffs in 1962, hoping to prepare for Irish entry into the EEC. The Anglo-Irish Free Trade Agreement signed in 1965 kept the country on the path toward opening up the economy to the outside world. The agreement made it possible for Irish manufactured goods to gain tariff-free access to the British market and also allowed cattle and butter greater access to the British market. Dublin agreed to reduce tariffs on British goods by ten per cent per year until free trade was achieved in 1975.

It would be wrong to underestimate the impact of the 'First Programme for Economic Expansion' implemented during Seán Lemass's premiership. There is no denying that, in the midst of a worldwide economic recovery, Ireland's economy expanded as it never had before. Growth rates of four per cent were double those that were called for in the initial plan. Ireland's economy grew at a time when the economies of much of the developed world were also witnessing significant expansion. One observer commented that it is important to understand how changes in economic policies coincided with this global expansion benefiting the Irish economy: 'There was no reason why the Irish boat should not rise on the international tide, and more than the British boat did, unless the Irish themselves changed their navigational tactics.'[41]

The success of the First Programme of Economic Expansion, which covered the years 1959–63, was not matched by the second, more ambitious plan. The Second Programme covered 1964–70. It was complicated by Ireland's failure to gain entry into the EEC and a number of industrial disputes that further hindered the government's effort to engineer and encourage additional growth. However, the experience of developing a rational plan that would co-ordinate national resources was an important and healthy development. Perhaps more importantly, the success of the First Programme gave a tremendous boost to the national psyche, as noted by Terence Brown.

> Most Irish people would still identify 1958–63 as the period when a new Ireland began to come to life. Most associate the success of those years with a renewed national self-confidence that continues to sustain the country even in its present vicissitudes.[42]

Government policies developed by T. K. Whitaker and supported by Lemass succeeded in taking advantage of the rising tide and expansion of worldwide trade.[43] The subsequent economic growth of the 1960s was uneven. However, it slowed emigration, provided jobs, cars, and televisions, and slowly improved the standard of living for many Irish citizens.

CHAPTER 2

Lemass and Northern Ireland

One historian of Ulster has maintained that when Seán Lemass became Taoiseach, he 'abandoned the overt irredentism of previous governments' although he 'preferred to say nothing about Northern Ireland at all.'[1] This portrayal of Lemass suggests an uninterested Taoiseach, unwilling to tackle the difficult questions that the border issue presented. Another historian has argued the opposite, maintaining that Lemass was the first Irish leader to have a 'Northern policy'.[2] This thesis has been supported by another observer, who maintains that, as Taoiseach, Lemass initiated an active policy of political revisionism in regards to Northern Ireland.[3] Another historian cautions that his initiatives were not a sharp departure from the policies pursued by his predecessor, Eamon de Valera. This argument points out that before his retirement from politics, de Valera had tried to engage Unionists in Northern Ireland and had made overtures to London in an attempt to address the issue of partition. Instead of seeing Lemass as a revisionist pioneer, this argument suggests that the Taoiseach simply adapted quickly to rapidly changing circumstances while remaining committed to the goal of a united Ireland.[4]

To understand these contradictions, and to try to untangle some of the conflicting signals Lemass often transmitted, one needs to examine how Lemass's ideas about partition evolved during his long political career. There was never a clear break or departure from his commitment to end partition; thus it would be wrong to suggest that Lemass moved abruptly from the role of hostile anti-partitionist republican to that of conciliatory moderate during his political career. However, under Lemass, the government embarked upon a more nuanced approach to the issue of partition and Dublin's relationship with what Irish governments had tradition-ally referred to as the 'six counties'.

Lemass differed from his predecessors by making a careful though concerted effort to engage with the Northern Ireland Government at Stormont. Previous governments had used international venues, such as the Council of Europe, to try and embarrass the British Government by denouncing London for fostering the evils of partition.[5] What was known as the 'sore thumb' policy receded under Lemass and was eventually discarded. Instead a cooler, more moderate presentation of established policy was pursued. The call for economic co-operation as a way to build bridges with Northern Ireland was a hallmark of Lemass's tenure of office. Admitting that there was a complex Unionist dimension that had to be acknow-ledged was part of the new strategy. De Valera had on occasion admitted that Unionists had real fears that needed to be addressed in any settlement of the partition question. However, this theme gained a new resonance under Lemass as part of a comprehensive policy of engagement with Northern Ireland.

Although a change in emphasis is discernible in Lemass's views on Northern Ireland in the mid-1950s, throughout most of his career Lemass had followed the traditional Fianna Fáil line by simply denouncing partition. In May 1949 while addressing an anti-partition meeting in Tipperary, Lemass proved that he was not immune from using inflammatory rhetoric when discussing the division of the island:

Independence will still need to call upon the capacity for high endeavour and unrestrained patriotism that one finds in Tipperary – perhaps even for another contribution from their undoubted store of honour.[6]

This may be seen as a romantic 'call to arms' by a Tánaiste suscept-ible to the nationalist passion produced by a Fianna Fáil political rally. However, once he became Taoiseach, Lemass demonstrated that he was not a republican ideologue obsessed with the issue of partition. Under Lemass, the rhetoric that had characterised previous Fianna Fáil governments became more muted in its condemnation of the division of the country.

Lemass has been judged a pragmatist, a reputation he rightly deserves. His pragmatism enabled him to disengage from both the economic and political constraints of Sinn Féin ideology embraced by Fianna Fáil since 1926. Indeed, he illustrated a degree of flexi-bility during the IRA's 'border campaign' that proved he was not opposed to short-term compromises on partition. He raised the idea of repartitioning the island with British officials at the height of 'Operation Harvest' in September 1959. At that time British *chargé d'affaires*, Gurth Kimber, visited Lemass to express his government's concern about the violence that had taken place along the border. Lemass responded by explaining that the govern-ment was doing all it could to combat the IRA and suggested that redrawing the border might be a short-term solution to the disorder plaguing the frontier:

I told him that these incidents occurred in areas like Co. Tyrone and Fermanagh which were incorporated in the Six Counties against the wishes of the majority of their inhabitants and that while redefining the border would not lessen our desire to see Partition ended, it would remove some of the tensions.[7]

The notion of redrawing the boundary between North and South impressed neither Kimber nor the British government.

The Irish economy showed signs of growth in the first half of the 1960s, which provided Lemass with a degree of confidence that encouraged him in his overtures to Northern Ireland. Although Captain Terence O'Neill took the first step by inviting Lemass to Belfast in 1965, the visit was made possible by the campaign launched by Lemass when he first became Taoiseach. From the start Lemass made it known that he wanted to develop a dialogue with Stormont, and on a number of occasions he invited O'Neill's predecessor, Lord Brookeborough, to visit Dublin. This courting of the Unionist government met with London's approval and support.[8]

As a leader obsessed with improving the performance of the Irish economy, Lemass was well aware that economic development would not take place in Ireland without an active government willing to take chances, even to risk failure. He knew that the failed practices of the past needed to be discarded and that age-old policies of protection and opposition to foreign investment were counter-productive. Likewise, if any progress was to be made in addressing the problem of partition, Lemass recognised that he would have to make policy revisions to try to gain tangible results. In political terms, as in economic terms, practices of the past, which had proved unsuccessful, had to be revised. Although the *means* had changed, the ultimate goal of re-unification had not.

Lemass openly admitted that his government was committed to the principle of a united Ireland, but he believed that other means could be employed to achieve this elusive goal. John Horgan traces the change in Lemass's thinking to 1955 while Fianna Fáil was in opposition. At the time Lemass was chairman of the Standing Committee on Anti-Partition, and in this capacity he forwarded a draft report of the committee to de Valera, who promptly shelved the document. The report had called for the government

[to] maintain and strengthen, wherever possible, all links with the Six County majority, especially economic and cultural links, to encourage contacts between people of both areas in every field, and to demonstrate that widespread goodwill for the Six County majority can be fostered by such contacts.[9]

Although his speeches sometimes lapsed into traditional Fianna Fáil anti-partitionist rhetoric, again and again Lemass returned to the theme that economic co-operation between Dublin and Belfast was essential, as it would help foster better relations between the two parts of Ireland. According to Lemass, greater economic co-operation would improve the economies of both jurisdictions and better the lives of all citizens.

Lemass's 'Northern policy' was a clear and definite departure from the not so recent past. Rather than simply ignore the 'six counties', Lemass believed that trying to find common ground on economic issues was a more appropriate way to address partition.

The policy that evolved under his direction might be described as one of constructive engagement. It was designed to encourage dialogue with Belfast in the hope that the two states could co-operate on issues that were mutually beneficial. The policy was complicated from the start, in that it was developed by a state whose constitution claimed jurisdiction over the 'six counties' that made up the province of Northern Ireland. The situation was further complicated by the fact that Lemass was trying to engage with a regime that had institutionalised discrimination against as much as one third of its population. The nationalist community in the province was divided and, for all intents and purposes, politically impotent. This was a community for which Fianna Fáil liked to think itself responsible. Fianna Fáil had a complex and often tense relationship with nationalists north of the border. The party's disposition towards Northern nationalists was in many respects paternalistic. Lemass was frustrated by divisions within the nationalist community and by his inability to engage with the Northern Ireland Government.

Because Lemass was committed to improving the Irish economy, the notion of advocating economic co-operation as a means of thawing relations with Stormont made a great deal of sense. He was well aware that there were substantial issues of economic co-operation worth exploring, and he hoped that economic development might entice a reluctant Stormont into exploring those areas where co-operation could be mutually beneficial. He hoped collaboration in economic matters would transcend the political difficulties that polarised the two administrations. Lemass believed economic co-operation might one day lead to the reunification of the island, maintaining that the entire island would inevitably be drawn into a trading bloc with Europe and that the rigidity of borders throughout Europe would be softened.

Before becoming Taoiseach, Lemass frequently denounced partition as an injustice that had been imposed by the British. He argued that London could remedy the situation by making a commitment to withdraw from the province. This was the standard Fianna Fáil rhetoric that had been applied to the partition question since the foundation of the party. Because Lemass was the government minister charged with overseeing economic development, his speeches often argued that the economic difficulties that confronted Ireland were compounded by, if not caused by, partition. In a 1953 speech to the American League for an Undivided Ireland the Tánaiste spoke of Ireland's long struggle against oppression and foreign domination. He embraced traditional republican language, explaining that generation after generation 'saw in foreign rule the never-failing source of all the ills from which the Irish people suffered'.[10] Lemass maintained that much had changed in Ireland since independence, asserting that 'poverty, squalor and ignorance are retreating before the strength and determination which the Irish people are directing the task of nation building'.[11]

Lemass further complained that economic progress had been retarded by the immoral and unconscionable policy of partition. Although the economic consequences were not always apparent, he assured his audience that

> These economic consequences are felt in the whole of the Island, in the partitioned north-eastern counties perhaps more keenly then elsewhere. The ending of partition would give the whole nation new strength to promote its progress – progress which enjoyed in every part of it.[12]

Lemass was, of course, preaching to the converted as he moved from the economic argument to more standard anti-partition rhetoric. In praising the work of American activists, Lemass argued that work had to continue:

> to get a more widespread understanding that Irish Partition is not merely an internal Irish problem but a wrong perpetuated by one country on another, in contravention of every principle of justice to which righteous men subscribe and something which must be rectified before the world's conscience can be at ease about it.[13]

This address and other similar speeches are interesting for the emphasis not only of the immorality of partition, but also for the economic argument that is woven into the critique. The same theme of economic retardation caused by the evils of partition was expressed when Lemass toured North America in 1953. He addressed the National Press Club in Washington DC, and once again explained the challenges that lay ahead for independent Ireland:

Our work is being seriously impeded by the persistence of partition . . . When the British Government of thirty years ago conceived the idea of partitioning Ireland they were probably not very concerned for the Irish people, north or south, but we who can see these consequences appearing and reappearing from day to day are very much concerned about them.[14]

On occasion Lemass attempted the difficult task of balancing the economic critique of partition with an appeal for investment. In Ottawa he argued against the 'economic absurdities' of partition while at the same time encouraging Canadian firms to invest in Ireland, where they 'may feel certain that they will be warmly welcomed in the expectation that closer commercial relations between the two countries will be mutually beneficial'.[15]

On becoming Taoiseach, Lemass declared that he hoped a new era of goodwill could be established between the two parts of the island. When interviewed by the *Belfast Telegraph*, he answered a number of difficult questions about Dublin's policy regarding the North. Responding to a statement made by the Prime Minister of Northern Ireland, Lord Brookeborough, Lemass argued that Ireland was one country and that his government was committed to eventual unity. He dismissed as 'fiction' the notion that Ulster was British and clearly explained his immediate goals:

Our aim is the reunification of the Irish people and the abolition of the memory of their past dissentions. We think of it as the coming together again of the members of a family who have been divided by disputes and misunderstandings . . . I have no illusions about the strength of the barriers of prejudice and suspicion which now divide the people, but, given goodwill, nothing is impossible. Meanwhile better relations can be fostered by practical co-operation for mutual benefit in the economic sphere.[16]

Lemass illustrated that on constitutional grounds he had not departed from de Valera's concept of how a post-partition Ireland could be governed. He maintained that in a united Ireland the North would still enjoy autonomy, as Dublin could accept an arrangement within given parameters:

> ... along the lines of continuing the six-county administration as at present, with a transfer to an all-Ireland Parliament of the functions now exercised in relation to the Six Counties by the Parliament of Westminster. This proposal appears to me to conform to realities. I am well aware of the importance and fears in the minds of Six Counties Protestants that, in an all-Ireland State, they would have in some way, an inferior status or be subjected to disadvantages because of their religion. Those fears are unfounded, but I recognise that they must be met; and that the retention of a separate Parliament, with the powers of the present, would be one way.[17]

This proposal was not a new initiative; it had been presented by de Valera in the past and had its roots in the 1921 republican cabinet. However, the style and delivery of the message were quite different to what they had been in the past. Lemass was anxious to address the majority in Northern Ireland directly through the Belfast paper. He was anxious to emphasise that he understood the fears of Irish Protestants.

Brookeborough and younger politicians in the Unionist establishment rejected these overtures. A young, ambitious Brian Faulkner responded by telling a rally in Newtownhamilton, County Armagh, that the Taoiseach's statements did not impress Unionists: 'Let it be clearly understood that we do not consider that there is an "Irish problem" as far as we are concerned.'[18] He also argued that if the Dublin government was serious about better relations, it would formally recognise the constitution and parliament of Northern Ireland and crack down on the IRA 'who cross our border to murder our citizens and destroy our property'.[19]

A short time later Lemass explained to the Dáil why he wanted to establish a dialogue with the Prime Minister of Northern Ireland. He made it clear that discussions with Stormont could result in a trade agreement, which would benefit manufacturers in Northern Ireland. These businesses had their access to the Republic impeded by restrictive tariff barriers. Lemass seemed to be addressing not only Stormont but also the business community in Northern Ireland when he asked rhetorically:

> Are there possibilities for a combination of effort in the field of tourist trade, an all-Ireland promotional campaign which would benefit the whole country? In both the north and south vigorous efforts are being made to attract and develop industrial projects. Could these efforts be co-ordinated with mutual advantage? Are there problems arising in cross-channel shipping which would be worth joint examination?[20]

The rationale outlined in this speech defined Lemass's Northern Ireland policy for the remainder of his term in office. In spite of the cold reception that Brookeborough displayed toward the proposals, Lemass proved tenacious.

The resistance of the Unionist establishment to these overtures was based on the suspicion that Lemass was not in fact advocating a new policy of co-operation. Many Unionists considered him a traditional nationalist, the proverbial wolf in sheep's clothing waiting for the opportune moment to swallow a distracted Ulster. In a debate at Stormont, Brookeborough explained his rejection of the Taoiseach's plea. This co-operation talk was 'only the thin edge of the wedge, as the object was that . . . [Northern Ireland] should be absorbed by the twenty-six. He could not contemplate that for a moment'.[21] The Taoiseach's efforts to encourage a dialogue with Lord Brookeborough were thus met with rejection – and the disdain of Stormont's ideologically rigid Prime Minister. In trying to engage Brookeborough, Lemass encountered a man who had illustrated an unambiguous hostility toward the Catholic minority in the province.[22]

This animosity is evident in correspondence between Brookeborough and the Rev. F. C. Gibson of the Presbyterian Church in 1951. The correspondence is instructive, as it illustrates the difficulty Lemass had in engaging Northern Ireland's Prime Minister. Gibson communicated on a regular basis with the Prime Minister, expressing the concerns of the Vigilance and Rural Problems Committee, an organisation he chaired. This committee had been established with one goal: to keep property out of the hands of Roman Catholics in Tyrone and Fermanagh, two counties in Northern Ireland with Catholic majorities. The committee was especially concerned with preventing large residences and estates from being purchased by Catholics, considering such transactions 'an additional menace to the maintenance of our Protestant population and Parliament'.[23]

Gibson wanted the government to purchase properties that were at risk of falling into Catholic hands. He explained to Brookeborough that he was particularly concerned that the Catholic Church was purchasing these properties, often older mansions or estates, for schools, convents or residences for religious orders. This was a cause for concern for Gibson and the Prime Minister, as it was clearly understood that these Catholics were likely to use the property vote to which they were thereby entitled. Gibson made this clear by asserting that 'the Pope has . . . ordered that all nuns, monks, etc. to vote in elections and as we know the nuns in Clogher Convent in a body voted in the recent election and we can see the danger that may arise from this quarter'.[24] Brookeborough, a native of Fermanagh, shared Gibson's concern for the stability of the Protestant population.

Brookeborough ordered Stormont's Department of Finance to look into acquiring some of the properties in question, hoping that they could be used as government offices or schools. After conferring with Maynard Sinclair, the Northern Ireland Minister of Finance, Brookeborough wrote to Gibson, explaining that he was sympathetic to his concern and that he appreciated the work his committee had done to try to 'prevent properties falling into the wrong hands'.[25] The Prime Minister maintained that the government would do what it could but cautioned that combating what he termed Catholic 'infiltration in towns and cities' was problematic for the government.[26] He encouraged Gibson to work with other groups that had been established to contain Catholics and to form 'one big organisation' that might 'achieve better results'.[27]

One might be inclined to dismiss this episode as one of sectarian paranoia on the part of Gibson and Brookeborough. However, eight years later the papal nuncio, Monsignor Riberi, called on the secretary of the Department of External Affairs, Con Cremin, in his Dublin office. The meeting illustrates that Gibson and Brookeborough had some justification in fearing that the Catholic Church might prove to be an agent in accelerating the 'infiltration' that caused such Unionist consternation. Cremin sent a confidential memorandum to Lemass detailing his discussions with the papal nuncio:

The Nuncio . . . expressed the view that the best policy we could adopt to end partition would be one of quiet and peaceful penetration. He went on to say that it seems to him that it would be worthwhile endeavouring to bring about conditions which would, in time, lead to a preponderance in the Catholic population. On the assumption that the Catholic birth-rate is higher than that of the Protestants and, on the further assumption that the birth-rate in the country is generally higher than in the towns, it would, he felt, be worth examining whether one might not assist Catholics in the Six Counties to acquire land. Such a policy would, of course, have to be pursued quietly. Those interested in the maintenance of the status quo within the Six Counties would, naturally, tend to react against the policy but the more quietly things are done the greater the prospects of obviating such a reaction.[28]

Monsignor Riberi did not offer to finance the 'quiet and peaceful penetration' he advocated. Nevertheless, the fact that the official representative of the Roman Catholic Church suggested that the government pursue such a policy is extraordinary. Cremin reported to Lemass that he had politely responded to the nuncio that the suggestion was, 'an interesting one, adding that I thought that something of this kind had been considered before. The great difficulty . . . would be whether the course of action envisaged would be practicable.'[29] Lemass ignored the nuncio's suggestion.

In spite of Lemass's best efforts, Lord Brookeborough announced that he was not interested in the appeals made by the Taoiseach and continued to ignore Dublin's attempts to initiate dialogue. The Prime Minister rejected calls by Lemass for a meeting without preconditions, and explained his position to the Northern Ireland House of Commons:

I am not prepared to take any action which would weaken our links with the United Kingdom: that is our economic strength, and to join with the Free State would not solve any of the problems we have got. The south is anxious about its economic position. It thinks now, having failed to bully or to blackguard us to join up with them, honeyed words will draw us in. Neither honeyed words nor anything else will do that.[30]

The only way that the Prime Minister would meet with Lemass was spelled out clearly: 'If the Éire Prime Minister would do as I suggest, [that is,] accept the constitution of Northern Ireland, then I am quite prepared to meet him.'[31]

Unless Lemass formally recognised the government of Northern Ireland, Stormont would not even consider co-operation between the two jurisdictions. This was true even if the price for non-co-operation financially punished the citizens of the province. This was made clear by events that took place in March 1959. At that time Northern Ireland's Minister of Commerce had broached the subject of 'a regional free trade arrangement between North and South' at a cabinet meeting.[32] He informed the cabinet that discussions had already taken place with officials in London – implying that the British had not objected to the scheme. The minister explained that before proceeding he wanted to 'ascertain the views of Ministers' on the 'political implications' of such a move.[33] It became clear quite quickly that this proposal could not be accepted:

> Strong objections were voiced by the Minister for Home Affairs on the ground that it was a first step towards turning Ireland into one economic unit; it would create a form of customs union from which Great Britain would be excluded and on this account would be highly objectionable.[34]

At the time of this debate Brian Faulkner, the future Northern Ireland Prime Minister, was serving as Minister of Home Affairs, and, at this period was an ardent, uncompromising and ambitious Unionist. As far as Faulkner was concerned, the notion of agreeing to any type of union with the Irish Republic was something that the government of Northern Ireland could not, under any circumstance, countenance – even if it meant that commerce in the province would suffer. The Minister of Commerce argued in vain that a trade agreement with the Republic would 'benefit Northern

Ireland manufacturers' who 'stood to make substantial gains'[35]; he therefore urged that the proposal 'not be turned down without the fullest consideration'.[36] The cabinet ultimately concluded: 'that the proposal for limited free trade with the Republic could not be supported on political grounds.'[37]

It is worth noting that although Stormont was opposed to any thaw in relations with Dublin in the absence of formal recognition of the Northern Ireland parliament, trade associations in the province made their own overtures to Dublin. The Ulster Furniture Association opened private negotiations with the Irish government, asking for a reduction in tariffs for goods manufactured north of the border. Lemass encouraged these low-level talks and instructed his government to accommodate the northern businessmen.[38]

In October 1959 Lemass gave one of the most significant speeches of his political career at the Oxford Union. He and the Prime Minister of Northern Ireland were invited to address the Oxford Union to debate the issue of partition. Brookeborough declined, however, explaining that:

> Northern Ireland's position within the United Kingdom was settled nearly forty years ago and can now only be changed by the parliamentary will of her people. In these circumstances [I do] not feel it would be a fitting for ... [me] to join the debate.[39]

A future Secretary of State for Northern Ireland, Patrick Mayhew took the place of the absent premier. Lemass's speech, entitled 'One Nation', articulated his vision of the way forward on the question of partition. The speech clearly presented the Taoiseach's opinion that a dialogue between Dublin and Belfast could be made easier if the British government offered its encouragement. Lemass argued that London could help by issuing a formal policy statement maintaining that it would not stand in the way of Irish unification:

We would, indeed, regard it as a very useful contribution to the
solution of the practical problem of ending it if the British Government would say: We would like to see it ended by agreement amongst
the Irish. There is no British interest in preventing, or desiring to
discourage you from seeking agreement.[40]

The Taoiseach outlined his government's desire to engage with
Northern Ireland by emphasising his determination to identify economic issues that could bring the two jurisdictions together. Lemass
quoted Prime Ministers Asquith and Churchill and King George
V's speech at the opening of the Northern Ireland Parliament in
1921, asserting that each saw Ireland as one nation that should not
be divided. Lemass was forthright in arguing that his government
desired a united Ireland and that co-operation on issues of trade
might be the start of a long journey towards unification. Moreover,
Lemass made it clear he did not have a hidden agenda:

I have not disguised my hope that economic co-operation would
eventually bring about this result; but quite apart from any views one
may hold about the eventual reunification of Ireland, is it not plain
commonsense that the two existing political communities in our small
island should seek every opportunity of working together in practical
matters for their mutual and common good?[41]

Lemass complained about the economic hardships that he believed
had been aggravated by partition. He speculated as to why his
overtures to Stormont had time and again been rejected:

Perhaps this is because they fear that evidence of the practical value of
combined action might lead, in time, to a growing recognition, in
Northern Ireland, of the artificial nature of the existing political
division.[42]

He exhorted the absent Lord Brookeborough to realise what was good for him and his fellow 'partitionists'. Lemass also sounded a note of understanding – a note that had not been part of the de Valera tune played so often on the partition issue. He understood that unity would mean changes in the constitution that his predecessor had drafted:

> We recognise, however, that the fears of Northern Ireland Protestants still exist and that it is unlikely that they could be removed by assurances of good intentions alone, no matter how sincere or how authoritatively expressed. An arrangement, which would give them effective power to protect themselves, very especially in regard to educational and religious matters, must clearly be an essential part of any ultimate agreement.[43]

Lemass once again outlined the qualified 'federal' solution to partition that he had mentioned in his interview with the *Belfast Telegraph* (July 1959). He emphasised that he understood that London had legitimate security concerns that had to be addressed by Dublin in any effort to resolve the partition question. He implied that Irish membership in the North Atlantic Treaty Organisation was not out of the question for a reunited Ireland. He returned to this theme on a number of occasions, especially when trying to prepare the ground for Ireland's application into the EEC.[44]

The speech was not a major departure in Irish government policy concerning partition. John Horgan rightly points out that this was not a new initiative and that 'his ultimate objectives in relation to Northern Ireland differed not a whit from de Valera's'.[45] The notion of Stormont continuing to exist but subservient to Dublin merely restated a concept that had been suggested by republicans, as early as 1921, as a possible solution to the vexing constitutional question of unification. No new proposals had been raised as to the constitutional solution that might bring about change. No concrete recommendations were aired concerning how the 1937 constitution might be amended. Many Unionists regarded de Valera's constitution, which recognised the 'special position' of the Catholic Church and forbade divorce even for non-Catholics, as sectarian. Articles 2 and 3 of the document, which claimed juris-diction over Northern Ireland, were regarded as irredentist.

However, the speech was important because it set a marker defining Lemass's 'Northern policy'. The statement that Unionists had legitimate fears that had to be overcome with more than pleasant words implied that constitutional changes would have to be made to try to encourage progress. Later in his career Lemass established a 'Constitutional Committee' to consider how the constitution might be modified to encourage North–South relations. He was a member of the committee that recommended deleting the contro-versial language concerning the 'special position' of the Catholic Church and abolishing the prohibition of divorce for non-Catholics. The Constitutional Committee also advocated substituting the claim on the territory of Northern Ireland with the following statement: 'The Irish nation hereby proclaims its firm will that its territory be reunited in harmony and brotherly affection between all Irishmen.'[46]

There were other revisions in the strategy developed to engage Stormont that departed from the policies that had failed so miserably in the past. In another significant policy speech on Northern Ireland that took place in July 1963 in Tralee, Lemass once again admitted that Unionists had legitimate fears that had to be conciliated. The fact that the Taoiseach insisted that Fianna Fáil always recognised these fears as legitimate is open to question. Nevertheless he admitted that these fears were real. Before Lemass's Tralee speech, Brookeborough had once again rejected an overture from the

Taoiseach, demanding instead that Dublin formally recognise the constitution of Northern Ireland and the legitimacy of Stormont. Lemass dismissed this rejection as a 'gimmick, an excuse for inaction'.[47] He understood, however, that it was impossible to recognise officially the legitimacy of Northern Ireland. However, in Tralee Lemass carefully extended the type of qualified recognition that he believed was appropriate: 'We recognise that the Government and Parliament there exist with the support of the majority in the Six-County area — artificial though that area is.'[48] Mentioning the words 'recognise' and the 'Government and Parliament of Northern Ireland' in the same sentence was a significant gesture to Unionists and an extraordinary statement for a Fianna Fáil leader.

Lemass made other efforts to try to improve relations with Northern Ireland. His desire to quietly change the way in which the entity north of the border was defined created a mild controversy at home but also indicated an effort on Lemass's part to find ways to thaw the frosty relations between North and South. His decision to instruct the civil service to refer to the state as Northern Ireland instead of 'the six counties' was a small gesture, perhaps one that was applied unevenly. It was an important gesture just the same. This issue of terminology may seem trivial, but it was significant that the civil service should recognise Northern Ireland by its name.[49] It should be pointed out that when quietly advocating this change in nomenclature, Lemass did not want to alienate cabinet colleagues, such as Frank Aiken, who were uncomfortable with the implied recognition of the Stormont government.[50] The Taoiseach was uneven in his own use of the term, but he certainly pressured Radio Éireann, Telefís Éireann and others to refer to the province as Northern Ireland. He tried to distance himself from this policy in the Dáil and illustrated a pragmatic

ambivalence in responding to a query about terminology from his
Minister for Finance, Jack Lynch. Lynch asked if Finance should
use the term 'Northern Ireland' or 'the six counties'. Lemass
responded: 'I have no strong views either way.'[51]

Lemass continued to attempt to engage Unionists in Northern
Ireland in spite of the refusal of Brookeborough and his associates to
reciprocate. A correspondence between Lemass and Ernest Blythe,
an Ulster Protestant who had embraced Irish nationalism, offers an
insight into the thinking of the Taoiseach during this unilateral court-
ship. Blythe had joined the Irish Republican Brotherhood prior to
the Easter Rising and later served as a minister in the Cumann
na nGaedheal Government from 1922 to 1931; he had earned a
reputation for encouraging draconian measures against republican
'irregulars' during the Civil War. After leaving politics, he became
the managing director of the Abbey Theatre from 1941 to 1967.

Blythe wrote to Lemass after visiting relatives in Northern
Ireland. He told the Taoiseach of how little things had changed in
the province, and how he was struck by the sectarian nature of
politics that characterised Northern Ireland. Blythe argued for a
radical change in Dublin's attitude toward Northern Ireland.
He believed that Dublin's Northern policies had been counter-
productive and only encouraged polarisation within the province.
Blythe made it clear that he did not think it wise for the Taoiseach
to mount a political offensive with its emphasis on economic co-
operation. He argued that Unionists 'saw through' what he defined
as a transparent effort to undermine the status of Northern Ireland.
Blythe challenged the Taoiseach's assertion that as Europe moved
toward a tariff-free zone, partition would become impracticable.
He complained that Dublin's emphasis on the inevitable blurring
of borders in Europe with the advent of the EEC, only succeeded
in further alienating Unionist opinion.

Blythe called upon the Taoiseach to formally recognise the government of Northern Ireland, arguing that it was the only responsible course to adopt. His language in calling for recognition was quite blunt:

> After all, if we want to co-operate with any man either in business or politics we should not, whatever his origin, keep on saying or implying that he is a bastard and should have been strangled at birth.[52]

Blythe argued that recognition of Stormont and a 'toning down' of criticism of the regime would ease the fears of the Unionist community. The inability of the state to recognise Northern Ireland was, according to Blythe, responsible for the sectarian nature of politics in the province, a point he was concerned to stress when addressing the Taoiseach:

> If at an early date we find ourselves able to abandon hostility and attempts at pressure, then even the Northern Nationalist party, which depends for its survival on the existence and exploitation of Catholic grievances will not be able to keep general politico-religious segregation alive and so will not be able to maintain Lord Brookeborough or his like permanently in power.[53]

The Taoiseach wrote back to Blythe, making it clear that he shared many of the concerns that the Ulsterman had expressed. Lemass once again outlined the arrangement he believed made the most sense for ending partition. He maintained that he saw no difficulty in 'maintaining a separate parliament in the north-east with powers equivalent to those exercised by Stormont'.[54] He repeated his vision of a federal solution where an all-Ireland parliament in Dublin would act as the mother parliament for Stormont, effectively granting Northern Ireland Home Rule. He recognised that this solution was not attractive to Unionists, but once again indicated his belief that it was London that was holding up progress:

> I do not expect that there will be any modification of their attitude in this respect unless the British Government say, in public, what many of them are prepared to say in private, that it would be regarded by them as a desirable arrangement.[55]

When he first became Taoiseach, Lemass told the British ambassador that he believed that it was a mistake to pursue an anti-partition policy through the agency of the British government. However, it is clear that he still saw a solution to partition as requiring at least an initial push from London. Lemass rejected Blythe's call for Dublin to give formal recognition to Northern Ireland:

> I have never been fully able to understand what is meant by 'recognising the legitimacy of the Northern Government'. If this expression is intended to convey that they represent the majority in the Six-County area, this is no difficulty. If it means that the Northern Government is seen as having a permanent future, within an all-Ireland Constitution, this is not a difficulty either. If it means a judgement on their historical origins, this is a different matter. It seems to me that when Brookeborough speaks of recognition this is what he has in mind – acceptance of the two-nation theory, or at least a confession that, because of the religious division, partition was only right and practicable solution to the problem.[56]

The Taoiseach continued by drawing attention to his numerous efforts to encourage co-operation between North and South:

... without seeking to impose any pre-condition of acceptance of any historical theory, or advertence to the fact that, while we do not conceal our hope that co-operation will lead in time to an acceptance of the concept of unity, they for their part say this can never be. It is my belief that the Common Market will compel co-operation on these terms.[57]

Many commentators have mentioned the fact that a general changeover in the personnel of Irish political leadership followed Lemass's succession as Taoiseach. In the Republic both Labour and Fine Gael parties experienced changes in leadership. Shortly after Lemass became Taoiseach, James Dillon replaced Richard Mulcahy as leader of Fine Gael, and Brendan Corish replaced William Norton as leader of the Labour Party. What is often forgotten is that a similar 'changing of the guard' took place in Northern Ireland. In Belfast an energetic and more moderate Terence O'Neill replaced the elderly Lord Brookeborough, who had clung tenaciously to power for 20 years. This change enabled Lemass to preside over a short-lived, but very real, thaw in North—South relations.

Captain O'Neill, unlike his predecessor, was interested in trying to transform Northern Ireland economically and politically. His twin aims were to modernise Northern Ireland and to 'build bridges between the two traditions within the community'.[58] Marc Mulholland's 2013 biography successfully captures the complexities of Northern Ireland's most controversial premier: a premier who ultimately failed to realise these goals. Although O'Neill was certainly more sympathetic to the Catholic minority than his predecessor, his disposition towards Catholics was also paternalistic. After his fall from power he tried to explain how difficult it had been for him to convince Protestants that Catholics would behave better if they had good jobs. His often-quoted comment on the minority population in the province illustrates his distance from the Catholic community:

It is frightfully hard to explain to Protestants that if you give Roman Catholics a good job and a good house, they will live like protestants because they will see neighbours with cars and television sets; they will refuse to have eighteen children. But if a Roman Catholic is jobless and lives in the most ghastly hovel, he will rear eighteen children on National Assistance. If you treat Roman Catholics with due consideration and kindness, they will live like Protestants, in spite of the authoritative nature of their Church.[59]

O'Neill initially maintained the Brookeborough line against meeting or negotiating with Dublin unless the Irish Republic formally recognised the constitution of Northern Ireland. However, Lemass and O'Neill were soon engaging with each other indirectly through a series of conciliatory speeches. Nine months after becoming Prime Minister O'Neill prepared a memorandum for new British Prime Minister Sir Alec Douglas-Home. The memo was written for a meeting between the two Prime Ministers in November 1963. In this document, O'Neill addressed the uneven but evolving relationship between Belfast and Dublin. He referred to the speech Lemass had made at Tralee, where the Taoiseach had given what might be described as informal recognition to the government of Northern Ireland:

Although this statement fell short of the constitutional recognition which Northern Ireland has always sought from the Republic, its general tone was regarded as not unfriendly.[60]

O'Neill explained that he had responded favourably to a subsequent call by Lemass for co-operation with Northern Ireland on issues beneficial to both jurisdictions. However, he expressed concern over what he clearly regarded as a certain regression on the part of the Taoiseach. He complained about remarks made by

Lemass during a state visit to Washington. O'Neill was upset that the Taoiseach had brought up the issue of partition and had called for the British government to make a statement that 'there would be no British interest in maintaining Partition when Irishmen want to get rid of it'.[61]

Although Lemass's Washington discussion was not by any means a departure from the policies that Lemass had had hitherto pursued, O'Neill was offended. He was also annoyed when the Taoiseach returned from his North American trip and announced to the press that the effort to encourage practical co-operation between Dublin and Belfast would lead to a 'total reassessment of the partition question'.[62] Lemass had, of course, made this a cornerstone of his 'Northern policy' during his Oxford Union speech, and it had been accepted and embraced by Fianna Fáil in its 1959 Ard-Fheis. At this juncture O'Neill, like Brookeborough before him, saw Lemass and his initiatives as simply old wine in a new bottle, telling the British Prime Minister:

> It is evident, therefore, that Northern Ireland is now confronted with the old anti-partition campaign conducted in a new, more sophisticated way. Its objects will be to propose measures of co-operation by practical means, but with constitutional ends, and to isolate Northern Ireland from the rest of the United Kingdom by achieving recognition of partition as solely an 'Irish' issue.[63]

O'Neill's complaints to the British Prime Minister demonstrate that statements made by Dublin concerning the 'resolution' of partition continued to fuel anxiety in Unionist Ulster. He implored the British government not to encourage or welcome any change in the constitutional status of Northern Ireland. When O'Neill met the British Prime Minister, Sir Alec Douglas-Home, the concerns and complaints articulated in the memorandum were not discussed.

The two men did talk about the possibility of IRA activity along
the border, and O'Neill sounded a note of sympathy for Lemass
that would not have been appreciated by more militant elements in
his own party. O'Neill claimed that 'he would be the first to admit
that Mr Lemass might be unable to take any effective action'.[64] At
this meeting, the British Prime Minister encouraged his Northern
Ireland counterpart to engage with the Taoiseach. Douglas-Home
told O'Neill that he had met Lemass when he worked in the
Commonwealth Office. Notably, O'Neill later recalled in his
autobiography that the British Prime Minister 'expressed the hope
that I would be able to meet him [Lemass] at some suitable date, a
sentiment with which I wholeheartedly agreed'.[65]

It is clear that, in spite of the difficulties expressed in O'Neill's
formal memorandum to Douglas-Home, progress was slowly
being made and would set the stage for the meeting that had been
endorsed by the British Prime Minister. The British government
was interested in encouraging the rapprochement it saw emerging
between the two jurisdictions in Ireland. Moreover, Downing
Street appreciated the efforts it saw emanating from Dublin and
tried to encourage O'Neill to reciprocate.

Press reports underscored the *détente* developing between
Dublin and Belfast. In March 1964, while addressing a Canadian
audience, O'Neill explained: 'Time is a great healer, and since
Eamon de Valera, Prime Minister of Southern Ireland, has passed
from the scene the new leaders have improved the outlook.'[66]
Although O'Neill warned Lemass that the constitutional status of
Northern Ireland was not up for discussion, he did indicate a
willingness to address other issues. He carefully downplayed the
importance of cross-border co-operation: 'Both Mr Lemass and I
will show our patriotism in a much more relevant way by striving
to better the lot and increase the prosperity of the people within
our respective jurisdictions.'[67]

Throughout 1963 Lemass had been pushing his ministers to identify areas where Dublin could co-operate with Belfast. By November, in anticipation of an informal meeting between civil servants from North and South, the cabinet reported that 56 areas had been identified.[68] However, in spite of some efforts to maintain momentum in communications between Dublin and Belfast, no real progress was made until 1965. In the meantime tension grew within Northern Ireland as nationalists were offended when the government announced that a new university for the province would be built, not in Derry, but in the market town of Coleraine. The decision to build a new city, Craigavon, further strained relations in the province and caused concern in Dublin.

Relations between Dublin and Belfast were also complicated by friction that developed between moderate nationalists in Northern Ireland and the new Stormont Prime Minister. The leader of the Nationalist Party, Eddie McAteer, travelled to London to meet with members of the Labour Party to advocate that a formal commission be established to investigate discrimination in the province. This effort was supported by the Irish government, which assisted the Nationalist Party by helping to document the widespread discrimination that had become institutionalised in Northern Ireland. O'Neill denounced the efforts of McAteer and his party, who he complained had 'taken every opportunity to run down their native province'.[69] He argued the traditional Unionist line that discrimination was, if not a myth, at least a vastly overrated issue. The Prime Minister claimed that the reports that were being presented at Westminster were slanderous and argued that 'we should condemn those who carry unbalanced and malicious accounts to Great Britain and elsewhere'.[70] He also denounced the support that the Irish Embassy in London had given to the McAteer group, especially the fact that the embassy had arranged a press conference for the Nationalist Party delegation. This was denounced as a 'tasteless and impertinent intrusion into our domestic affairs, and inconsistent with that policy of mutual respect from which better relations might develop'.[71]

However, even in this period of strained relations, Lemass was advising cautious ministers to take the risks needed to encourage dialogue. With the encouragement of Lemass, Erskine Childers, the Republic's Minister for Transport and Power, attended a meeting with Unionists at Castleblayney, County Monaghan, in April 1964. The meeting was arranged by the United Societies of Castleblaney, which hoped to encourage co-operation between Dublin and Belfast. The conference included Nationalist and Unionist politicians from both sides of the border. The meeting had been arranged to enable an open and frank discussion about partition and to encourage dialogue between the two adminis-trations. Childers reported that the 'proceedings were conducted in a friendly spirit and the audience was well behaved'. [72]

A short time later Childers advised Lemass that he had been invited to a similar conference to talk to a group that would include Unionist members of the Stormont parliament. Childers asked for the advice of the Taoiseach on attending, aware that the meeting might be disrupted by 'a handful of people determined to make trouble, which would get very wide publicity'.[73] Childers was also worried that his fellow T.D. Richie Ryan might be provoked by the Unionists and create an awkward situation. Childers wanted to be certain that 'Ryan would keep his temper and not indulge in histrionics, which would have absolutely no purpose and would get us nowhere'.[74] Lemass wrote back to his anxious cabinet colleague, encouraging him to attend:

> On the whole I think meetings of this kind are useful. If you are satisfied as to the bona fides of the organisers, then, notwithstanding the risks you mention, I think you might agree to attend.[75]

In spite of the political difficulties that developed throughout 1964, in January 1965, Lemass travelled north to Stormont for his famous visit with Terence O'Neill. The Prime Minister of Northern Ireland had seized the initiative and finally responded to the relentless pressure exerted by Lemass to embark on a more open policy of dialogue and co-operation. O'Neill explained that having now been in office for almost two years he had decided to invite Lemass to Stormont: 'I felt sufficiently secure to take some bold initiative in order to break Northern Ireland out of the chains of fear which had bound her for forty-three years.'[76]

Dr T. K. Whitaker and Jim Malley, O'Neill's private secretary, arranged the encounter. The meeting was kept secret, because Lemass and O'Neill did not want what Lemass described as 'extraneous influence brought to bear on us before the meeting'.[77] Lemass understood that there would be critics of the visit, and that some of the more 'green' members of his party would be uncomfortable with his journey north – many of them, indeed, regarding it as *de facto* recognition of the government of Northern Ireland. Lemass rejected this criticism in a generous statement that emphasised the importance of reuniting people, rather than territory:

> If we are ever going to have unity in Ireland, we are going to have to bring all of the people of the country into it and to cherish them all equally. You cannot admit only to membership of an Irish Republic those who are in agreement with our political philosophy. You have to bring them all in. Unity means just that – bringing the people together. It is not a matter of territorial acquisition: it is bringing the situation about where the people of Ireland come together and decide, notwithstanding their previous history and attitudes, to try and make a go of their country as one unit.[78]

The Stormont visit generated tremendous publicity and encouraged a great deal of hope that a new era in North-South relations had
dawned. O'Neill travelled to Dublin a short time later, and Lemass
succeeded in encouraging the Northern Ireland Nationalist Party
to enter Stormont as the official opposition party. However, events
on the ground were moving in another direction by the time that
Lemass's successor, Jack Lynch, travelled to Belfast in 1967.

CHAPTER 3

Lemass and the British

The British government regarded the appointment of Seán Lemass to the office of Taoiseach as a positive development. London looked forward to working with the new Taoiseach and hoped that under Lemass's leadership better relations could develop between London and Dublin. For Lemass it was imperative that his government maintain a cordial relationship with London for a number of reasons. The Taoiseach knew that a healthy Anglo-Irish accord was critical if Ireland was to pull itself out of the economic torpor that enveloped the country throughout the 1950s. Lemass was well aware that past intercommunications between London and Fianna Fáil administrations had often been troublesome, and he quickly demonstrated that he was committed to improving relations with Britain. Further, he understood how critical the British market was to the health of the Irish economy, especially in the area of agricultural exports.

Lemass was committed to improving and expanding trade with Britain. Once he became Taoiseach, he proposed that both Ireland and the United Kingdom adopt of policy of free trade, dismantling all tariffs and duties between the two countries. His interest in free trade became more pronounced in the wake of Britain's failure to become a member of the European Economic Community (EEC) in 1963. Once Britain's application was rejected, the Irish government, realising that it could not enter the ECC without its largest trading partner, suspended its own application. Lemass was disappointed that Ireland's entry into the EEC had been delayed, but predicted that by 1970 the country would be a member of the community.[1] In spite of this setback he remained a committed 'Europeanist' and looked forward to the day when Ireland would be part of an integrated European community. In the meantime the Taoiseach was keen to negotiate a bilateral free-trade agreement with the United Kingdom.

Boosting the Irish economy by means of a trade agreement was not the only reason why Lemass wanted to improve Dublin's relationship with London. He believed that London could encourage Unionists in Northern Ireland to engage Dublin in meaningful discussions. He hoped that initiating a productive dialogue with Belfast would lead to an improvement in the dysfunctional relationship that characterised North–South relations. Lemass also remained hopeful that the British government could be convinced to issue a statement stipulating that London would not hinder the reunification of Ireland if a majority of the country's population, on both sides of the border, expressed a desire to end partition.

Though he occasionally lapsed into traditional republican rhetoric for party-political purposes, such instances were rare. On the whole he was careful to insure that in his public pronouncements little offense was offered to the British government. This chapter will examine Anglo-Irish relations in the Lemass era by considering how the Taoiseach and British governments worked to improve contacts, and how Lemass tried to influence British policy towards Northern Ireland.

In Dublin, the British Embassy watched the 1959 presidential elections with a great deal of interest. The observations of embassy staff offer insight into how the British viewed political events in Ireland during this time of transition. In a letter that accompanied a long dispatch to the Colonial Office, the British *chargé d'affaires*,

Gurth Kimber, explained that it had become obvious that de Valera would win the presidency. However, Kimber did not regard it as inevitable that Lemass would assume the leadership of Fianna Fáil and become the next Taoiseach. He reported to London that there was a possibility of a power struggle pitting Frank Aiken against Lemass. In such a scenario, he predicted that Minister for Finance, Dr James Ryan would emerge as a compromise candidate.

Later, when it became clear that Lemass would in fact be the next Taoiseach, the embassy leadership was clearly relieved. It was firmly of the opinion that Lemass was the best person for the job. However, George Kimber was not convinced that the Irish constitution was powerful enough to contain the wily founder and mentor of Fianna Fáil. He believed de Valera would continue to exert influence from Áras an Uachtaráin:

> There is, I fear, a general belief (and in some quarters fear) that Mr de Valera will continue to try to run the party and the country from Phoenix Park. If that is so, Mr Lemass's appointment is all to the good, as he is a man of both determination and ability who is much more likely to make up his own mind rather than 'run to the Park for his instructions' as, some foretold, would be the case with Mr Aiken.[2]

Kimber's dispatch underscored the embassy's concern implying that, owing to the former Taoiseach's 'obsession with power . . . combined with Mr de Valera's political skill and confidence in his own infallibility, it may be that he will continue to exercise great, but perhaps more discreet influence upon the policies of the Government'.[3]

Aiken was also clearly seen as a problem: the British believed that he was anglophobic and had been sympathetic to Nazi Germany during the war.[4] There was, therefore, genuine relief when Lemass had been chosen as the successor to de Valera. Kimber's report to

London maintained that although it was tempting to speculate what sort of political changes might take place in Ireland following the departure of de Valera from government:

> I will refrain from doing this, not least because nothing ever does seem to change here in the 'timeless west'. Nevertheless, we may perhaps hope that, under Mr Lemass, the conduct of relations between our two countries may be slightly less frustrating than in the past. The real 'nigger-in-the-woodpile' [*sic*] is, of course Mr Aiken, and we have no idea how much he will be allowed his head (to change the metaphor) under the new regime.[5]

The dispatch provided an evaluation of Lemass that is worth quoting at length, as it illustrates a certain respect the British had for the new Taoiseach. It also provides evidence demonstrating how British policy-makers understood politics in Ireland during this time of transition. Kimber described Lemass as:

> a man of broader outlook and considerably more intelligence than many of his colleagues. He is much more practical and less visionary than Mr de Valera and is generally regarded as the leader of the 'progressives' in the Fianna Fáil party ... Although perhaps he is a little lacking in the arts and graces of a political leader, he has shown himself an able and energetic administrator ... As Tánaiste, he has continued to concentrate on his job of economic development and trade promotion, and unlike so many of his colleagues, he has sought to deal in his speeches with these tangible subjects instead of wandering over the barren (but, to Irish eyes, attractive) fields of ancient wrongs ...
>
> We should ... welcome his appointment as we can know that he will be prepared, so far as political expediency allows, to deal with relations between our two countries upon the basis of realism and mutual self-respect. It cannot, of course, be said that he has anything of Mr de

Valera's magic or popular following, and time alone will show whether it will be possible for his party machine to build him up into the 'father figure' required of the Taoiseach in this country where personalities still count for more than policies. Unfortunately, he too was involved in the 1916 Rising, and the subsequent 'Troubles', and we shall have to wait a few years yet before this country is at last given a Prime Minister who was not himself entangled in the destructive divisions of our time.[6]

The British ambassador to Ireland, Sir Alexander Clutterbuck, watched the de Valera–Lemass transition closely, and forwarded his observations to London. He was clearly delighted to see de Valera leave office after dominating Irish politics for years and welcomed the accession as Taoiseach of a more amenable figure. The tone of the ambassador's memorandum is remarkable for its overt hostility towards de Valera:

> Indeed, it is impossible not to pity him. For over 35 years now he has stood for and sought to promote three main objectives, the reunion of Ireland, the economic self-sufficiency of the country and the restoration of the Irish language not merely in schools but in every-day life. In none of these three aims has he succeeded. The last two are hopelessly unrealistic, and this is now being even more widely acknowledged . . . Yet there he is, a prisoner now in Phoenix Park, 76 and half blind, feeling that his life work is incomplete, too old to change or even to grapple with it any more, a dictator bereft suddenly of power, thinking the same thoughts and employing the same arguments as he did 35 years ago, and no longer appreciating the implications of the new age in which we live.[7]

Clutterbuck believed that Lemass had to navigate carefully along a perilous course, as the old guard in Fianna Fáil could sabotage his reforming efforts. However, it is clear that the British were delighted at the transition under way in Ireland. Clutterbuck was pleased with the new Taoiseach's desire to improve North–South relations. He recalled a conversation he had with Lemass when the two men discussed Northern Ireland:

> Mr Lemass said quite frankly to me that he fully realised on looking back that a great number of mistakes had been made by the Government here in relation to the North; these he would work to rectify. It was a totally wrong conception, for instance, that this country should bring pressure on the North, whether direct or through Britain or the United Nations. Any such pressure would be self-defeating, as it would only serve to harden opinion in the North, instead of bringing the day of reunion nearer.[8]

Clutterbuck's report runs counter to the Taoiseach's efforts to encourage London to issue a statement indicating that it would not stand in the way of unification if people on both sides of the border supported the ending of partition. It also contradicts Lemass's attempt to persuade London to encourage Unionists at Stormont to open a dialogue with Dublin. His remarks to the British ambassador suggest that Lemass was trying to find a balance between different views of partition: between regarding it as a problem created by the British, and thus repairable by London, or as an issue to be addressed between Dublin and Belfast. Lemass planned to pressure London lightly by employing more subtle tactics couched in moderate terms.

Lemass understood that London's support for his long-term goal of reunification was critical. He also knew that Belfast had to be part of any solution – and that simply ignoring Stormont by defining partition as an Anglo-Irish problem was unrealistic. However, accepting that Belfast had a legitimate role to play in trying to resolve the 'Irish question' was problematic because it raised the issue of recognition. As Taoiseach, Lemass would need to engineer a delicate policy which would ensure the active involvement of Stormont without formally recognising the legitimacy of the 1920 Government of Ireland Act. The 1920 Act had partitioned Ireland and created the state of Northern Ireland and its parliament.

In London the Commonwealth Office agreed with the reports emanating from British officials in Dublin, viewing Lemass as a practical leader with whom London could work. It predicted that an administration led by Lemass would herald 'a gradual shift of policy towards a more practical approach to current problems, including particularly the cultivation of friendlier relations with the North'.[9] The British government believed that if de Valera retired from active politics relations among London, Dublin and Belfast would improve. Sir Gilbert Laithwaite, Under-Secretary of State in the Commonwealth Office, had served as the UK's ambassador to the Irish Republic from 1950 to 1951, and was in a unique position to evaluate the new Taoiseach. In July 1959 he prepared a memorandum for his colleagues in the Commonwealth office predicting an improvement in Anglo-Irish relations:

> He is a practical, down to earth man, I think well disposed toward us (not for historical but for practical reasons) . . . Already Mr Lemass, though in very general terms, has adjured his people to stop talking about partition and concentrate on improving relations with the North, and he added (something that would not have been practicable earlier) that he would be very glad to see Lord Brookeborough in Dublin, if Lord Brookeborough cared to come down.[10]

In 1959 Ireland was outside the two trading blocs that had developed in Europe, the European Free Trade Association, which included Britain, and the European Economic Community, which included France. Lemass was committed to gaining entry to the EEC but knew that Ireland could never join without its largest trading partner, Britain, also becoming a member. In these circumstances, he travelled to London to try to negotiate a bilateral trade agreement with London that would make it easier for Irish agricultural exports to gain access to the British market.

In order to strengthen Lemass's position, the Commonwealth Office was encouraged by Laithwaite to try to deal sensitively with the Taoiseach in the impending trade talks:

> I do feel strongly that in these circumstances we need to be at pains in the trade negotiations that lie ahead to bear in mind the possible political importance, in terms of closer relations with the Republic, of not giving the Irish too raw a deal . . . They are at the same time a poor country, essentially dependent on agriculture, and any concessions that we make which affect their agricultural economy could be of economic as well as political importance.[11]

Briefing papers were prepared for the British Prime Minister, Harold Macmillan, before he was to meet with the Taoiseach. In the documents Lemass was described as 'sensible, courageous and cool headed, a man of affairs with his feet on the ground, and it is to be hoped that in his present office he will bring, as far as is practically possible, a more realistic approach to relations with the United Kingdom and Northern Ireland'.[12] His republicanism was measured as more palatable as he was 'less rabid on the subject of partition than most Republican politicians'.[13]

Lemass impressed Macmillan. The Taoiseach was a straightforward advocate for Ireland and did not hesitate to explain in clear terms what it was he sought from the British Prime Minister. According to a Foreign Office record of the meeting, Lemass was:

perturbed by the economic state of Éire. Now that her goods were to
be excluded from much of the continent by high tariffs, he had to seek
some other outlet for Irish trade. He had therefore come over to
England to offer protection [and] expanded opportunities for British
goods in Éire in exchange for a better market for Irish agricultural
goods in the United Kingdom. He himself was not opposed to some
diminution of the Irish tariffs which at present protected home
industries so that they would have to face some competition.[14]

Lemass was frank, admitting that the problems he faced at home
were formidable. He did not appear optimistic about encouraging
Ireland's farmers to embrace change; he made it clear that he
regarded agricultural modernisation as problematic owing to the
immutable nature of Irish farmers. As far as the Taoiseach was
concerned, these farmers were an obstacle to the expansion of the
agricultural sector because they were 'very conservative and did
not adapt to new methods at all readily'.[15]

Significantly, partition was not central to this first meeting
between the two prime ministers, though Lemass touched upon
the subject in the context of a more general discussion of economic
development. He told the British Prime Minister quite bluntly
that economic development was critical for Ireland and that the
border complicated his desire to improve the Irish economy:

[Lemass's] main object was to organise some economic development
in Éire and for this it was very important to have a united country. The
population was now only three million and was declining; Éire was the
only country in Europe in which this was happening.[16]

Lemass further conveyed to Macmillan that he hoped to improve
relations with Belfast:

The great thing was to create a better atmosphere and [Lemass] hoped
that this could be achieved by economic relations and by arranging to
talk more with the leaders of the north. Improvement could only be
got, brick by brick, and it was his intention to lay a few of these bricks.[17]

The Taoiseach's futile efforts to court Lord Brookeborough,
the Prime Minister of Northern Ireland, were watched with great
interest by London officials. Reports from the British embassy in
Dublin explained that Brookeborough had continually rejected
Lemass's overtures, complaining that the Irish government refused
to recognise the constitution of Northern Ireland. The embassy
approved of Lemass's efforts to develop a dialogue with Belfast, and
was encouraged by Dublin's decision to use of the term 'Northern
Ireland' instead of 'the six counties'. The embassy reported that the
change in terminology was part of a concerted effort to assuage
Unionists on the issue of recognition. British officials were under no
illusion that this would have any real impact upon Unionist opinion
although the British embassy did see some benefit:

> This will perhaps go some little way towards meeting the Northern
> Ireland Government's prerequisite for official contacts, i.e. recognition
> of the Constitutional status of Northern Ireland.[18]

The trade talks succeeded in producing a modest trade agreement
with London in April of 1960. The agreement did not satisfy
Lemass, however, and his government remained committed to
negotiating a more comprehensive bilateral trade agreement with
London.

In March 1963, Lemass met once again with the British Prime
Minister, Harold Macmillan, to address the failure of both countries to become members of the EEC. The British embassy had
informed London that in spite of the setback the Irish were

'wholeheartedly set on getting into the EEC and they are corres-pondingly depressed at the failure of [the] British application'.[19] The embassy reported:

> [Lemass] hoped that the recent events could be regarded as no more than a check in the movement towards European integration. For their part the Irish would continue to shape their domestic policy on lines which they hope will make it easier for them to enter into a European Community should this all become possible later. For example, present intention was to introduce a second round of voluntary tariff cuts on 1st January 1964.[20]

When Lemass met Macmillan the two prime ministers addressed failure of both countries to become members of the EEC. The pending application for British and Irish entry into the EEC had delayed the exploration of a more comprehensive trade agreement between London and Dublin. Now, in the wake of the rejection, Lemass and Macmillan discussed what sort of policies should be developed in the aftermath of the failed Brussels negotiations. Lemass made it clear to Macmillan that he wanted once again to explore the possibility of a comprehensive free trade agreement with London. He reminded Macmillan that in the past the Irish government had made proposals to improve trade, but that these efforts had failed owing to the pending EEC. application. Since circumstances had now changed, Lemass thought the time ripe for a comprehensive Anglo-Irish trade agreement.

Lemass told Macmillan he wanted a bilateral agreement with London, seeing it as offering more advantages for his country than membership in the European Free Trade Association. He under-lined the point that Ireland was the largest per capita consumer of British goods worldwide and emphasised his own interest in modernising and expanding the Irish economy. Lemass argued that,

The old days of a large tariff protection for Irish industries were over; the high tariffs had served its purpose. Industry no longer needs high tariffs and these should now be dismantled if possible.[21]

Following the advice of his staff, Macmillan decided to stall on the issue of an agreement; he told Lemass that 'Europe had been delayed but the attempt to create it should not be abandoned. We should certainly not jump into something different.'[22] Frustrated by Macmillan's uncooperative attitude, Lemass pressed his case for a trade agreement – stressing that it would be beneficial to both Dublin and London, and emphasising his government's willingness:

[to] contemplate giving expanding opportunities for British trade . . . provided that reciprocal advantages could be obtained. [Lemass] believed that a bilateral arrangement of this kind could be worked out without prejudices to the future of the Common Market.[23]

The meeting ended with the British Prime Minister agreeing that the matter 'should be studied'.[24]

Lemass returned to Downing Street one year later, in March 1964, and continued to push for a comprehensive free trade agreement. A briefing document prepared by Macmillan's staff outlined the manner in which Anglo-Irish trade had evolved since Lemass had become Taoiseach. The British government was not impressed with the proposals Lemass had put forward and believed there was little to be gained by continuing negotiations. With this in mind, Macmillan's staff advised:

The question is whether you should say something which will discourage Mr Lemass from expecting a favourable outcome or whether you should be non-committal and play for time.[25]

Macmillan knew that a very modest agreement was possible, but even a limited agreement could be problematic for a number of reasons. The Prime Minister was aware that British farmers, the Northern Ireland government, members of the Commonwealth and other European countries would complain if Ireland was given special consideration. In spite of the difficulties that an agreement would cause, important political considerations had to be weighed. Macmillan's staff advised the following:

> The general policy which Mr Lemass has been pursuing of bringing the Irish Republic closer to us politically is a welcome development of Anglo-Irish relations. An abrupt rejection of his ideas, impracticable though they have proved to be on examination, might damage his own position and impair this development. [26]

The Prime Minister was further advised that the best option was simply to stall the Taoiseach:

> Perhaps you could assure [Lemass] that we have been looking at his proposals with a full recognition of the political advantages to both of us of making some of them . . . You might stress that at this stage in the life of the present Parliament it is difficult to give full thought to these problems, and suggest that there should be no further Ministerial discussions for the present. [27]

When the meeting eventually took place, Lemass made his pitch for an Anglo-Irish free trade agreement: the British premier, for his part, remained cool. Macmillan pleaded for consideration of what he described as a 'double problem', stating that:

> the United Kingdom ['s] population was likely to grow to about 69 million by the end of the century. We wished both to give our own

producers some margin for growth whilst retaining a share of the
growth for our traditional suppliers . . . It was a question of making a
difficult adjustment between home producers and traditional suppliers;
we had to keep a certain amount of flexibility.[28]

In October 1964 Lemass encountered a serious setback to better
trade relations with the United Kingdom. On 26 October the
British government announced that it was unilaterally imposing a
15 per cent surcharge on all imports into the country in an attempt
to deal with a balance-of-payments crisis that was putting pressure
on the British economy. Lemass was clearly upset with London's
decision, describing it as an 'abrupt and unilateral termination of
existing trade agreements'.[29] The new Prime Minister, Harold
Wilson, met Lemass in London in November to hear his complaints
about the tariff. Wilson tried to placate the Taoiseach, explaining
'it was the intention of the British Government to reduce the
temporary import charges as soon as the balance-of-payments
position permitted'.[30] When the surcharge was reduced from 15
per cent to 10 per cent, Wilson wrote to Lemass to advise him of
the reduction. He explained that while reviewing the tariff, 'we had
your difficulties much in mind'.[31]

The British ambassador visited Lemass to deliver Wilson's
letter. The Taoiseach then told the ambassador that 'from our
viewpoint the objections to a levy of 10 per cent were as strong as
to one of 15 per cent and that the refusal of the British government
to eliminate from the scope of the levy certain goods of particular
importance to this country was disappointing'.[32] In spite of these
difficulties, negotiations aimed at hammering out a free-trade
agreement continued with the Wilson government. After much
discussion an agreement was eventually signed in December 1965.
Lemass later explained that the Irish efforts to secure an Anglo-
Irish free-trade agreement had continually been hindered by

British procrastination. According to the Taoiseach, this tactic changed when Harold Wilson became Prime Minister, because the British responded to the Irish initiatives by 'following it up with positive action'.[33] In many respects the agreement helped pave the way for Ireland's entry into the EEC. Lemass believed it was one of the most important initiatives his government had launched.

Lemass had reason to be pleased with his government's efforts to develop meaningful relations with London. The trade agreement was an important accomplishment for the Taoiseach. Although London did not issue a declaration stipulating that it would not stand in the way of Irish unity, Lemass knew that the dialogue he had established with Belfast in 1965 had substantially improved Anglo-Irish relations and had developed the channels through which more significant progress could be made in the future.

CHAPTER 4

Lemass and the Catholic Church

In the early years of the Irish Free State, W. T. Cosgrave, the head of the Cumann na nGaedheal government, enjoyed excellent relations with the Irish Catholic Church and the Vatican. Cosgrave established diplomatic relations with Rome in 1930 and emphasised his government's Catholic credentials in subsequent election campaigns. He made much of his government's Catholic connections in the tumultuous election campaign of 1932. The support that many clerics gave to Cosgrave's party in the 1920s and early 1930s greatly annoyed Seán Lemass. During a by-election in 1925 Cumann na nGaedheal received the backing of many influential members of the clergy. This prompted Lemass to attack the clerical influence that he saw as pervasive in Irish politics:

> The question of the political influence of the Catholic clergy, an influence that throughout our history has been used with uncanny consistency to defeat the aspiration of Irish nationality has to be faced sooner or later . . . Whenever the Irish people came within sight of achieving their national independence the full political power of the Church was flung against them, and forced them back. That political power must be destroyed if our national victory is ever to be won . . . We are opening a campaign now against the political influence of the Church. If we succeed in destroying that influence we will have done good work for Ireland and, I believe, for the Catholic religion in Ireland.[1]

Two years later, in 1927, Lemass was elected a Fianna Fáil deputy for Dublin City South – and was immediately confronted by the requirement that all members of Dáil Éireann swear an oath of allegiance to the British crown. Frustrated by his inability to take his seat in the Dáil, Lemass wrote to Edward Byrne, the Archbishop of Dublin, as a private citizen, asking for advice. One month after the election, on 8 July 1927, he told the archbishop that he was 'forcibly prevented from entering the Dáil Chamber' for refusing to abide by the constitution of the Irish Free State.[2] His query to the archbishop provides an opportunity to view Lemass in transition, moving from the fiery rhetoric of republican revolutionary to the moral ambiguities hindering the pragmatic politician:

Am I morally justified in taking the oath in Article 17 of the Constitution of the Irish Free State, seeing that I am publicly pledged to my Constituents, and privately determined also, to nullify, by every honourable means available to me, the authority of the British Crown and Cabinet in Irish Affairs?[3]

A note scribbled on the back of Lemass's letter indicates the archbishop consulted on this delicate matter with other members of the hierarchy during a meeting of the Synod:

The Bishops of the Standing Committee were strongly of the opinion that no answer . . . be sent on the grounds that an answer would involve the interpretation of the Oath which might be considered a 'casua major' for the Holy See . . . Whatever answer was sent would be used as a political weapon to the detriment of religion and the church's influence in Ireland.[4]

The archbishop's office wrote back to Lemass, informing him that Archbishop Byrne had gone away for a fortnight, but that he would 'look into the matter'. In the meantime the archbishop wanted to know 'if you wish for confidential advice between [him] and his spiritual son, or if it is your intention to communicate his answer to your political colleagues'.[5] Lemass replied: 'I did not consult my political colleagues on my intention to ask his advice with reference to the Oath of Allegiance. I would, however, prefer to be free to communicate his answer to them.'[6] The archbishop had little reason to look upon Lemass's request with much sympathy. He was a close friend of William Cosgrave and kept a signed portrait of the President on his desk.[7]

Two days after Lemass had initiated this dialogue, the Vice-President of the Executive Council and Minister for Home Affairs, Kevin O'Higgins, was assassinated while on his way to mass in Booterstown, County Dublin. O'Higgins's murder prompted the Cosgrave government to introduce legislation that convinced de Valera and Fianna Fáil to accept the oath and enter the Dáil. On 11 August 1927 Lemass entered the Dáil, took the oath and was admitted to his parliamentary seat. The archbishop never answered his moral dilemma.

From its beginnings Fianna Fáil had serious difficulties with the Catholic Church, and these did not dissipate until the party came to power in 1932. Once in power, however, Eamon de Valera set out to prove that he could beat Cosgrave and Cumann na nGaedheal at their own game. Gradually de Valera emerged as a leader who could work closely with the church hierarchy, as evidenced by the 1937 Constitution, which recognised the 'special position' of the Catholic Church and embraced Catholic social thought. However, this relationship with the church[8] was not always as smooth as has sometimes been suggested.[9]

As de Valera's principal lieutenant, Lemass illustrated a degree of ambivalence in his relationship with the Catholic Church. His 1925 attack on the insidious clerical influence contrasts sharply with his speech as Taoiseach at the Patrician Congress in 1961, when, 36 years after denouncing clerical influence in Irish politics he praised the church's role in society and noted the moral lessons of Patrick. Describing the teachings of Ireland's patron saint as the nation's 'unfailing guide', Lemass contended that they directed Ireland's foreign and domestic policy:

> To the best of our ability we have endeavoured to express these truths in the Constitution which we gave ourselves, to which all our laws and all of the regulations of our affairs must conform, and which stands under the invocation of the Most Holy Trinity 'from Whom is all authority and to Whom, as our final end, all actions both of men and States must be referred'.[10]

By 1961, of course, Lemass was a seasoned veteran of church–state confrontations, and had learned valuable lessons about working with the powerful Catholic hierarchy. Throughout the 1950s and during his tenure as Taoiseach Lemass avoided open conflict with the Church and tried to reach accommodation behind closed doors. By the time he became Taoiseach in 1959 Lemass understood that the church could easily jeopardise government initiatives. Experience taught him that the church wielded substantial political power and more importantly, was not afraid to use it. The political strength of the church convinced him to adopt a cautious, strategic approach on issues relating to church dogma. No matter how uncomfortable Lemass was with this situation, political pragmatism dictated that he work quietly with the hierarchy in order to avoid public controversy.

As a cabinet minister and Tánaiste during the 1940s and 1950s, Lemass tangled with the church a number of times and was occasionally willing to challenge individual members of the hierarchy whom he believed guilty of threatening to undermine government policy. However, the majority of battles engaged in by Lemass were temperate yet intense confrontations with the powerful Archbishop of Dublin, John Charles McQuaid. These conflicts concerned issues such as: health care, adoption and education.

One of his earliest confrontations occurred in 1944 when Lemass initiated a major public dispute with the church by openly criticising Michael Browne, the Bishop of Galway. Browne was the outspoken chairman of the Commission on Vocational Organisation, and a significant contributor to a controversial report issued by the commission. The report's conclusions were openly critical of Lemass and the Department of Industry and Commerce for ignoring advice offered by the Federation of Irish Manufacturers (FIM). As Minister for Industry and Commerce and as Minister for Supplies, Lemass was no stranger to the FIM; he had tangled with the organisation a number of times, and he had often criticised its members for being inefficient.

Accusing Lemass of arrogance and complaining that he had discounted the FIM's valuable suggestions, the commission claimed that he had 'committed a serious mistake'.[11] Lemass had little respect for the Commission on Vocational Organisation, regarding it as a gathering of uninspired amateurs who knew little about the complexities of government. He considered Browne's criticism both ill-informed and politically motivated. In responding to the report Lemass was scathing but impersonal:

> I have been unable to come to any conclusion as to whether the querulous, nagging, propagandist tone of its observations is to be attributed to unfortunate drafting or to a desire to distort the picture.[12]

Lemass dismissed the report as 'a slovenly document', clearly upset that the church had stepped beyond acceptable parameters in attacking government policy.[13] And 20 years later the dispute still rankled Lemass: even in 1966, he criticised the report as being a rushed and poorly produced document.[14] This incident however, – and the reaction it provoked – proved an exception. Throughout his career, as senior government minister and Taoiseach, Lemass was a pragmatic politician who sought to protect the government through effecting compromise and accommodation.

Later in his career Lemass learned an important lesson in the complexities of church–state relations by negotiating a Health Bill with John Charles McQuaid, the Archbishop of Dublin. McQuaid was a deeply conservative and highly controversial archbishop who was comfortable intervening in the political and cultural affairs of the nation when he believed issues of faith and morals were at stake. Historian Tom Garvin describes McQuaid as 'a kind of ecclesiastical dictator of the Dublin Archdiocese' noting:

> His influence was pervasive, affecting schools, housing developments, newspaper advertisements, marital relationships, university life and appointments, schoolteachers' employment and relationships between Catholics, Protestants and Jews. His word was law in large sections of the Catholic Church, parts of the civil service, Dublin Corporation, the university colleges and, of course, the primary and secondary school systems.[15]

The health legislation developed by Fianna Fáil brought the state into conflict with the church because the hierarchy feared the government would infringe upon matters it believed were the exclusive remit of the church. A similar bill, known as the Mother-and-Child Scheme, helped destroy the already fragile inter-party government in 1951. The legislation was designed to reduce infant mortality by offering free pre-natal and post-natal care to mothers and medical care to children. Originally developed by Fianna Fáil in 1947, the scheme became controversial when advocated by the

Minister for Health in the inter-party government, Dr Noel Browne. The hierarchy objected to the scheme on 'moral grounds' and found a powerful ally in the Irish Medical Association. The IMA, a formidable organisation that represented the interests of Ireland's physicians, was upset that the legislation would provide free care for mothers and infants without a means test. The IMA was able to cleverly exploit the fears of the Catholic hierarchy by maintaining the legislation would bring socialised medicine to Ireland.

In 1951 Browne's coalition partners refused to stand with him against the church and Ireland's physicians, thereby precipitating the minister's resignation and the failure of the legislation. The controversy was further ignited in a sensational manner when the *Irish Times* printed related correspondence between Browne and the hierarchy. A short time later, beset by internal problems, the inter-party government collapsed.

Archbishop McQuaid considered the failure of the Mother-and-Child Scheme a tremendous victory for the church:

> The decision of the Government has thrown back socialism and Communism for a very long time. No Government, for years to come, unless it is frankly Communist, can afford to disregard the moral teaching of the Bishops.[16]

During the ensuing general election Lemass met with Noel Browne in an effort to persuade the maverick TD, now an independent member of the Dáil, to support a minority Fianna Fáil government. During a bizarre secret meeting, which took place in a car on Harcourt Street in Dublin, Lemass persuaded Browne to back Fianna Fáil. The former Minister for Health respected Lemass and listened as the future Taoiseach assured him, stating: 'there's no bargain, no deal, but we'll try to give you a good health service.'[17]

Browne was impressed with Lemass's honesty and lent critical support to the fragile Fianna Fáil government.

When Fianna Fáil replaced the inter-party government in 1951 it found that its alternative Health Bill was problematic in the eyes of the church. Like its predecessor, the Fianna Fáil government encountered significant opposition within the hierarchy and the Irish Medical Association. Tension developed quickly in meetings between the hierarchy and the government, which was represented by Lemass and the Minister of Health Dr James Ryan. Moreover, at this critical juncture, the Tánaiste was acting on behalf of de Valera who was recovering from eye surgery on the continent. As the *de facto* head of government, Lemass held a number of meetings with McQuaid and members of the hierarchy who were intent on rewriting the proposed health legislation. These difficult negotiations provided a fundamental lesson in church–state relations for the future Taoiseach.

When the government published a white paper in July 1952 outlining their proposed bill, the hierarchy protested immediately. The church objected to the health scheme, fearing that its introduction would bring socialised medicine to Ireland. It was uneasy with the prospect of increased state control over the lives of citizens and upset that the proposal did not include a means test. The church hierarchy was also appalled at the prospect of the state offering reproductive care and sex education. As in 1951, an alliance of moral and monetary concerns was formed. The Irish Medical Association fiercely opposed the legislation and allied itself with the hierarchy. The IMA denounced the white paper for extending state control and providing free medical care to patients regardless of their ability to pay medical fees. On 6 September 1952 representatives of the IMA contacted the Archbishop of Dublin, asking for an 'urgent' meeting to discuss the white paper. McQuaid told the doctors that, in his opinion, 'the White Paper was open to very grave objections in its Mother and Infant provisions'.[18]

Two days later the archbishop asked Lemass to meet him, upset that the government was moving quickly on legislation that he believed threatened the moral fibre of Catholic Ireland. The archbishop later noted that, having received this summons Lemass dutifully 'called at once that afternoon'.[19] McQuaid told the Tánaiste that 'it was a grave pity that the Government had not consulted us about the white paper . . . [and] ventured to express . . . regret that the Government . . . gave the impression of wishing to exclude the Hierarchy from social legislation'.[20] McQuaid reprimanded Lemass for not consulting with the hierarchy on the white paper, complaining that the government was effectively confronting the church with a *fait accompli*. The archbishop feared that the new Fianna Fáil government was ready to fight an acrimonious battle like the one Noel Browne had waged the previous year. Furthermore, the archbishop made it clear that he held Lemass accountable as the acting head of government.[21]

According to McQuaid, 'Mr Lemass showed surprise, saying that Dr Ryan believed he was quite correct in the Scheme he had prepared. He personally was not very well acquainted with it.'[22] The Tánaiste did not openly challenge the archbishop but instead gave the impression of being sympathetic to the concerns of the hierarchy. Lemass's stance was never confrontational but rather accommodating, indicating that he was willing to work with the archbishop to find common ground. In fact, the Tánaiste quickly accepted McQuaid's demands and agreed that he would send Ryan to meet informally with him 'before doing anything further by way of implementation or discussion in the Dáil'.[23]

At this juncture the archbishop was pleased that Lemass was receptive to his advice. He reported to Archbishop of Armagh and

Primate of All Ireland, Cardinal D'Alton, that the meeting with the Tánaiste had gone well:

> The atmosphere, then, is more propitious than I had believed. In Mr Lemass we have a man of commonsense who greatly believes in negotiation with a view to settlement.[24]

One can sense that the archbishop viewed Lemass as a pragmatic politician who was going to co-operate with the church on the controversial legislation. McQuaid asked D'Alton to establish a committee of bishops to review the white paper. In doing so he referred to an earlier precedent, the episcopal committee that had been appointed by D'Alton to consider the government's Adoption Bill in January 1952. While the government was drafting this bill it invited a representative of McQuaid, Father Cecil Barrett, to review the legislation and offer the church's opinion. This clerical scrutiny was reflected in the bill that was introduced in the Dáil.[25] One commentator remarked that: 'The text of the bill bore out the closeness of the consultation, for regard was had to all the limits and safeguards for which the committee of the hierarchy had asked.'[26]

Evidently the Archbishop of Dublin was pleased that the church had influenced the adoption legislation and was confident that the process could be replicated with the impending health legislation. In asking D'Alton to establish another committee, McQuaid reported that 'The technique of the Adoption Bill worked with excellent smoothness and eliminated even the semblance of opposition.'[27] D'Alton agreed with the archbishop and an episcopal committee was quickly established to investigate the white paper, and formally submit its observations to the government. McQuaid chaired the committee, which included the Bishops of Cashel, Ferns, Galway and Cork.

Once the committee was established, McQuaid followed up on Lemass's earlier commitment and invited Ryan, the Minister for Health, to a meeting. Ryan's response to the Archbishop's invitation set a conciliatory tone: 'I gathered from Mr Lemass . . . that there was some misunderstanding of the provisions of the White Paper and it would be well to have cleared this up.'[28] However, far from being the informal discussion that Lemass had agreed to, the meeting turned out to be a much more formal encounter between the Minister of Health and the recently established episcopal committee. The negotiations proved to be extraordinarily difficult. The assembled bishops scrutinised the white paper line by line, listing detailed objections. In doing so, the bishops made it clear that they believed the proposed legislation threatened what they understood as Catholic social teaching. McQuaid struck a raw nerve when he addressed what he considered the most problematic part of the white paper. He reported that he 'firmly emphasised that it was quite contrary to Catholic teaching to give free [health] benefits irrespective of personal resource'.[29] McQuaid noted:

> The Minister showed himself quite uneasy at this stage. The Bishop's view very obviously worried him, but at no stage did he say he would not amend the section so as to satisfy Catholic social teaching. The Chairman suggested that he amend the section by allowing a subvention to those over £600 income, whose special circumstances required a subvention. This provision would in our view safeguard Catholic teaching.[30]

Ryan listened carefully to McQuaid, but did not make any commitments to modify the legislation. Instead, he promised to advise his colleagues of the hierarchy's concerns. The minister's failure to assure the hierarchy that the government would accept its recommendations greatly disturbed McQuaid.

A few days after this confrontation with the Minister, McQuaid reported on these events to the general meeting of the hierarchy. He warned the assembled bishops that the government had not been co-operative and might push ahead with the legislation. In view of such an eventuality, McQuaid advised the Irish bishops of the strategy that he proposed to pursue, in attempting to force the government to comply with the committee's demands. Unless the government accepted his committee's detailed amendments, McQuaid advocated issuing a statement condemning the government at an appropriate time, preferably during the committee stage of the bill, when it would become 'a test case for the conscience of Catholic deputies of every party'.[31] Although McQuaid assured the bishops that he would work to 'prevent any conflict developing', he was clearly willing to use the power of the church to intimidate the Dáil and its Catholic deputies.[32] The hierarchy and Cardinal D'Alton endorsed the archbishop's plan to appeal directly to the country by issuing a public statement condemning the legislation.

A short time after the meeting of the bishops, McQuaid met Lemass at a reception for the Catholic Truth Society and once again asked the Tánaiste to come see him. Dutifully Lemass reported to the archbishop's palace for what proved a 'frank and cordial' meeting.[33] McQuaid wrote a careful and detailed memorandum of the encounter: 'I went over the objections to the Mother and Infant Scheme of the White Paper, declaring that it was quite contrary to Catholic moral teaching to give free benefits to citizens in such a manner, irrespective of their needs.'[34] Lemass listened carefully; however, he explained to the archbishop that it would be politically difficult to scale back the legislation. Referring to the elections that had enabled Fianna Fáil to form a minority government, Lemass maintained, 'It is very hard to give less, when more has been publicly promised, especially as the trade unions will be expecting as much as they can obtain.'[35]

Lemass was in a precarious position: he was well aware that the Fianna Fáil government depended on independent deputies such as Noel Browne for its survival, and yet he did not want to cause a public crisis that would lead to the downfall of the government. The Tánaiste, as acting head of state, was under a great deal of pressure. He was caught between McQuaid's expectations that the government should accept as law the dictates of the church and the more secular pressures emanating from the Dáil, where he was trying to maintain a fragile minority government. Lemass, ever the pragmatic politician suggested the two sides find a compromise but the archbishop rejected this suggestion. Although he was by no means unsympathetic to McQuaid's position, Lemass refused to simply accept the dictates of the church, mindful of the political consequences that could result.

Lemass's refusal to accept the demands of the church greatly frustrated McQuaid, who once again complained to him about the failure of Fianna Fáil to consult the hierarchy. Although the arch-bishop considered playing his trump card – that is, releasing a public statement denouncing the legislation – the politically savvy archbishop held his fire: 'I did not [let] Mr Lemass . . . know the decision of the Hierarchy at its General Meeting, believing that it was much more useful to retain that weapon for future use, if the need should arise.'[36] For the time being, at least the church-approved weapon was held in reserve.

Even after meeting Lemass a second time, McQuaid was convinced the government was about to introduce the legislation he adamantly opposed. This was confirmed at the end of October 1952, when the archbishop reported:

I learned, secretly, and from a most trustworthy source, that at a meeting of the City of Dublin Health Authority, the Minister [Ryan] had used rude and forcible language, declaring that the Government was determined to put through the White Paper, and ordering an increase of 2/- in the (pound) for the Dublin rates, a very grave figure indeed.[37]

McQuaid was not only disturbed by this account received from one of his many confidential sources, but also upset by the suggestion of a tax increase. It was at this stage, in November 1952, that the IMA once again intervened and ultimately pushed the church to act. They released a statement to the press condemning the proposed legislation arguing that it was not in the best interest of the public. The IMA did not mention its own self-interest or the issue of infant mortality. Instead it argued that 'From the moral practical and financial points of view, experience has shown that such a course of events is to be utterly condemned.'[38] In the aftermath of the IMA declaration, the controversy only grew more intense, fuelled by media reports that indicated the government was about to forge ahead and introduce the legislation in spite of the objections raised by the church and the medical profession.

Alarmed by the increasingly public character of the controversy, the archbishop wrote an urgent letter to Lemass, which was delivered by hand to the Tánaiste. It was at this pivotal juncture that McQuaid threatened to use his secret weapon – the public statement condemning the government. Thus he confronted Lemass as the acting head of government:

You are very clearly aware that the Hierarchy has abstained from any comment, because the Scheme is being considered by the government, after representations have been made by the Chairman of the Episcopal Committee. But the long silence of the Hierarchy is open to grave misunderstanding, inasmuch as the Hierarchy can be regarded as lending assent to the provision of a free motherhood and

infant scheme. Hitherto, because of the indisposition of the Taoiseach,
I have refrained from even the appearance of pressing for consideration of our very grave objections to the scheme as unacceptable from
a moral view-point.[39]

Adopting a more direct and forceful approach, the archbishop
complained that he was tired of waiting for the government to
attend to his concerns. Moreover, he made it clear that he expected
Lemass to address the issues raised by the episcopal committee
even while de Valera was in Holland receiving medical care. He
demanded the following of Lemass:

> As Acting Head of Government, [you should] . . . consider whether it
> would not be possible and opportune to favour me with the assurance
> that, in the very near future, the Government will be good enough to
> accord full weight to the most serious moral objections that I have
> brought to the notice of the government.[40]

McQuaid knew that he now had Lemass in a very difficult position.
His urgent letter implicitly threatened to undermine Lemass by
suggesting that de Valera would have handled the entire matter
differently. Lemass was at this time trying desperately to hold
together a fragile minority government until de Valera was well
enough to return home to deal with the issue.

In a subsequent letter to the papal nuncio, McQuaid complained
about Fianna Fáil, stating 'one may never forget the revolutionary
past of that party. On so many occasions, the party was on the side
opposed to Episcopal directions.'[41] McQuaid identified a dangerous
liberalism in Fianna Fáil that 'must be incessantly watched.'[42] It is
clear that the archbishop longed for the more pliable inter-party
government and its conservative Catholic leader John Costello

whom he regarded with particular respect. McQuaid described Costello as:

> an excellent Catholic, but also an educated Catholic, in sympathy with the Church and the teaching of the Church. Nor was Mr Costello unduly worried about placating the Liberals and the Freemasons of the North or South . . . When the crisis came in the Mother-and-Child Scheme of Dr Browne, Mr Costello immediately and, when the need for declaration arose, publicly, made his own decision the decision of the Hierarchy.[43]

Unaware of McQuaid's scathing critique, Lemass responded to the archbishop's concerns, assuring him that the government was still working on the proposed legislation and listening to comment from various interested parties. He told McQuaid that once the Minister for Health had reported to the government, and before the proposed legislation was published, he would again communicate with him.

Given these controversial developments, it is hardly surprising that Lemass contacted the Taoiseach in Holland to explain the difficulties that had arisen. In reply de Valera acknowledged 'the great danger ahead in the White Paper' and advised the Tánaiste to meet with the hierarchy to review all of their objections.[44] The Taoiseach went so far as to suggest that the archbishop be asked to write his own draft of the proposed bill: 'This draft could then be examined from our point of view, and amended if necessary, until arriving at an agreed-upon text. That was more or less what happened in regard to the corresponding articles of the Constitution.'[45] In light of de Valera's suggestion another meeting was arranged between the Tánaiste and the episcopal committee. However, before it took place, the committee considered the political implications of the coming confrontation with Lemass. What becomes clearly evident in these deliberations is that McQuaid simply did not trust the Tánaiste.[46] His committee decided that, for the time being, it would not accept any of the amendments that Lemass might suggest:

> because of the general tenor of the White Paper as a measure tending to depart from Catholic social principles and because in view of the very proximate recess of the Dáil, we did not wish any expressions of our Committee to be used for purposes of political advantage and propaganda.[47]

McQuaid was a clever political tactician and understood the need for caution in dealing with Lemass. He did not want a repeat of the mother-and-child fiasco, and was careful above all to protect the church's image in society.

Such was the contentious environment when Lemass and Ryan returned to meet the episcopal committee. Again, they reviewed the proposed legislation line by line, addressing every item that the episcopal committee found objectionable. Not surprisingly the stumbling block arose when discussion turned to the question of free medical care to mothers and infants. The ensuing discussion took more than an hour. In an attempt to break the logjam McQuaid read out loud a 'statement of principle' that he had drafted with the committee. McQuaid had used this document, with little success, in a discussion with Lemass at an earlier meeting. However, on this occasion it appears that progress was made, as the Tánaiste suggested willingness to compromise. During these discussions McQuaid reported that 'Lemass's attitude was very surprising as he was clearly in complete good faith'.[48] According to a report prepared by the archbishop: 'The Tánaiste expressed his satisfaction and said he would like a copy of the statement of principles.'[49] However, Lemass still 'stressed the political difficulty of retrenching, after certain promises had been made in the White Paper'.[50] The meeting ended with Lemass assuring the episcopal committee that he would send the bishops the amendments that would be drafted.[51]

Despite Lemass's assurances, McQuaid still did not trust the Tánaiste. Events reached a climax in April, when the episcopal committee, fearing the government was about to push the legislation through the Dáil without incorporating its amendments, drafted a letter condemning the scheme and the government.[52] The letter was delivered to the national newspapers, with the exception of the *Irish Times*.[53] Just as the letter was about to be published, de Valera, back from eye surgery in Holland, succeeded in getting the hierarchy to withdraw it. The government quickly worked out an agreement that satisfied the hierarchy. The episcopal committee informed de Valera that it accepted the government's concessions and the amendments made to the bill. The 14 April letter condemned the legislation, and the Fianna Fáil government was withdrawn.[54]

Lemass fought in vain for a Health Act that would not include a means test. He demonstrated a willingness to engage the church hierarchy, and tried to live up to the commitment he had made to Noel Browne in 1951 when the two men had sat in a parked car in Harcourt Street. Browne concluded that in the end the hierarchy dictated terms that were 'accepted meekly by de Valera'.[55] Moreover, Browne complained that the legislation that emerged had 'emasculated' the original act.[56] His conclusions have been questioned by a number of observers; one has argued that 'despite these concessions, the amendments appear to be more of a victory than a defeat for the government'.[57] In the end Lemass accepted de Valera's decision to seek further accommodation with the hierarchy. In doing so, he displayed once again a certain degree of ambivalence when confronted with complicated political issues. Neither the Tánaiste nor the Taoiseach were interested in becoming embroiled in a public controversy with the Catholic Church. Lemass, the political pragmatist, understood that accommodating the church was an important part of maintaining political power.

Lemass's experience during the Health Bill negotiations had a lasting impact on him. The episode underscored the need for sensitivity in addressing issues that concerned the church. Throughout the 1960s as Taoiseach, Lemass avoided conflict and enjoyed good relations with the Catholic hierarchy. The lessons of 1953 clearly had not been forgotten.

In September of 1965, however, Lemass, now Taoiseach, asked Minister of Justice Brian Lenihan to approach the Catholic hierarchy on the delicate matter of reintroducing divorce for non-Catholics. Several factors underlay this initiative. Lemass was partly motivated by a desire to prove that Ireland was indeed a nation that respected religious diversity. He was also mindful of the criticism that was aimed at the government from Unionists in Northern Ireland. The approach, however, was rebuffed when the Chancellor of the Dublin diocese, Dr Gerard Sheehy, informed Lenihan that 'there would be violent opposition from the hierarchy to any proposal to allow for divorce in the State'.[58] Lemass knew that, if his government moved to allow divorce for non-Catholics, the leader of the 'violent opposition' would again be Dublin's formidable archbishop John Charles McQuaid. Given Lemass's earlier encounter with this adversary, he quietly shelved the initiative.

One year later, Lemass comfortable in his role as elder statesman, pushed for reform in church–state relations; reform that he could not have advocated earlier in his career. As part of his campaign to establish more friendly relations with Northern Ireland, Lemass sought to make a gesture towards Unionists in Northern Ireland by revising parts of the 1937 Constitution that he regarded as awkward examples of Catholic triumphalism. Viewed as particularly contentious were the articles that recognised the 'special position of the Holy Catholic Apostolic and Roman Church', embraced Catholic social teaching, and laid claim to Northern Ireland.[59] In 1966 the Taoiseach established an all-party committee of the Dáil to review the constitution, and to make recommendations on how it could be amended to be a more inclusive document. The review addressed articles in the constitution that concerned the Catholic Church, especially the issue of divorce for non-Catholics.

The committee recommended the amendment of Article 41 of the constitution, which stipulated that 'No law shall be enacted providing for the grant of a dissolution of marriage'.[60] It criticised the 1937 Constitution for:

> ignoring the wishes of a certain minority of the population who would wish to have divorce facilities and who are not prevented by securing divorce by the tenets of their religious denomination to which they belong.[61]

It suggested that the constitution went too far in embracing Catholic dogma for all of its citizens, regardless of their religion. The committee's report, in short, called for a more liberal social policy in keeping with the spirit of Vatican II.

Although the report was not submitted to the Dáil until after he left office, Lemass supported the reforms advocated by the committee. Lemass believed the suggested changes would make the 1937 document – and Irish society at large – less sectarian.[62] The church, however, demurred. While acknowledging the justice of the committee's call for removing language that referred to the 'special position' of the Catholic Church, the bishops rejected the recommendation that non-Catholics should have the right to a divorce complaining that the Constitutional Committee had not consulted the hierarchy. Cardinal Conway warned that:

> Once the first divorce law has been introduced it will be only a matter of time till it is extended to apply to everybody. I am sure that Irish husbands and wives will ponder very carefully on what the committee's

proposal to open the gates to divorce will almost inevitably lead to in terms of family life.[63]

This episode must have sounded eerily familiar to the elder statesman. As a veteran of church–state confrontations, Lemass understood that the political power of the Catholic Church had to be respected. Events in the past had taught him that disputes with the hierarchy could be exhausting, and ultimately could risk the political agenda one wanted to promote. Although Lemass supported the call for substantial revisions of the constitution, these battles would be left to future generations of Irish leaders.

In fact Northern Ireland Protestants had good reason to fear that their religious liberties would not be respected in a united Ireland. For many, the 1951 mother-and-child controversy proved the extent of clerical influence in matters of state south of the border. Indeed, a communication from Archbishop McQuaid to the papal nuncio Ettore Felici reveals the hostility of the hierarchy toward Protestants in Northern Ireland. McQuaid complained to the nuncio about an infamous editorial in the *Irish Times*, which, in the aftermath of Noel Browne's resignation, denounced the power of the Catholic Church in Ireland:[64]

> The outcry from Protestants in the North, following the unjust presentation of the Bishops' judgement by the Irish Times, is indeed typical. But what many fail to see is that the Protestants now see clearly under what conditions of Catholic morality they would have to be governed in the Republic.[65]

Archbishop McQuaid's sentiments could hardly be described as ecumenical. His statement illustrates that the Unionist community was justified in viewing the Catholic Church as a powerful, intolerant institution.

In spite of the fact that Lemass witnessed the church taking an active, often invasive, role in Irish politics, he was always careful to maintain publicly that the Catholic Church was never a real threat, never a force that intruded heavily into the realm of politics. In a series of interviews conducted by Michael Mills of the *Irish Press* in the winter of 1969, Lemass addressed church–state relations. When asked about the influence of the Catholic Church Lemass denied that there was excessive clerical influence at work in Irish affairs:

> As Taoiseach I never had the slightest problem in this regard, nor do I recollect any occasion when the Church tried to pressure me in any area affecting Government policy. Once or twice members of the Hierarchy came to me to express anxiety about certain minor developments that were taking place, mainly in the context of the appointment of individuals in whom they had not much confidence, but never to the extent of pressing for a change.
>
> I felt that they were expressing their concern as citizens with certain things that were happening but they never made any attempt to impose their views on me. Once or twice I was in doubt as to what the reaction of the Church might be to some proposals and I went along to discuss them with members of the Hierarchy, but this was merely to clarify my own mind. I felt the best course was to go to the fountain-head of Church authority rather then to go to some theological expert, to tell them that I had certain proposals and to ask them if they saw any objection to them. I do not recollect that there were any objections . . . We had to make certain that what we proposed would not be rendered nugatory by active Church opposition. I think that in the case of Dr Browne and his mother-and-child scheme that he just handled the affair ineptly as a politician.[66]

This is a remarkable statement by a politician who had tangled so often with the church, especially as Tánaiste. Two years earlier he had seen the recommendations of his constitutional committee denounced as 'dangerous' by the same church that he now defined as non-interventionist. Moreover, Lemass told Mills that he was optimistic about the future of church–state relations and denied that a future collision was inevitable:

> I think it is extremely unlikely at least. At the moment one could not even visualise the area in which it might arise. No I do not think it will happen. Not with the Church. You will get individual Bishops who will express views the Government cannot accept, and who will make criticisms of government, but we have never hesitated to hit back when this happened. I think this was good for the Bishops as well as for the government.[67]

Lemass learned to charter a safe, careful course with the Catholic Church during his long ministerial tenure and while Taoiseach. The fiery anti-clericalism of 1925 grew mute by the time he became Taoiseach. As Tánaiste, while 'standing in' for de Valera in 1953, he experienced very difficult negotiations with the Catholic hierarchy. These events had taught Lemass a valuable lesson. Although he might disagree with the pronouncements or policies of the church, it did not make political sense, in a conservative Catholic society, to publicly challenge that powerful institution. The maintenance of Fianna Fáil's political power in government and economic growth remained, as ever, his priorities. He was, in Irish terms, the ultimate practitioner of *realpolitik*.

CHAPTER 5

Lemass and the Introduction of Irish Television

By the time Seán Lemass made his most famous statement concerning Irish television being an 'instrument of public policy' the Taoiseach had been involved in shaping the form and structure of the medium in Ireland for close to a decade.[1] This chapter will consider the role that Lemass played in bringing television to Ireland in the last days of the de Valera government as Tánaiste (and Minister of Industry and Commerce) and while Taoiseach when critical decisions were being made about establishing an Irish television service. It will also consider his vision of the role television should play in Irish society. Throughout the 1950s an often times animated debate took place in Irish society and within both coalition and Fianna Fail governments about television and how a native service should be structured and introduced to the nation. During the decade a consensus developed within these governments, which maintained that because of the costs involved, television simply was impossible for the state to encourage or support. The 1950s were, of course, a difficult period which witnessed seemingly relentless emigration, high levels of unemployment and stubborn economic stagnation. In this climate the notion of starting up a television service did not have much support in government circles.

In spite of this there was an understanding at many levels of society that television was inevitable and that basic questions had to be confronted. Much of the discussion in government circles and in the press during this time revolved around the question of who would control an Irish television service and the programmes it would transmit. Therefore the issue of what structure Irish television would take became critical. From the outset the state looked to Britain and saw two options to choose from. The first was to set up a state owned and financed 'public service' modelled on the British Broadcasting Corporation (BBC). This attractive, though costly, option was popular for many who advocated exploiting the medium to provide educational and cultural programmes. There was a belief that an Irish public service could produce high quality educational material that would explore the complexities of Irish history and literature; support the native language; and generally reinforce what many regarded was a frail national culture. The alternative was to follow the example of the Independent Television Authority in Britain and grant an exclusive broadcasting license to a private firm. This option would not require government financing as television would be owned and operated by a corporation interested in making a profit by selling 'air time' to advertisers. As a market driven enterprise it would seek the widest possible audience for its underwriters and therefore feature predominantly 'popular' American and British programmes. What clearly emerged during this period was a debate between those who favoured a service that would be set up as an independent, commercial, entity, versus those who endorsed a more 'Reithian'[2] concept of a government owned and operated 'public' service. Those that supported the latter option maintained that both radio and television should uplift and educate the nation and not simply provide popular entertainment for the masses. Advocates of each of these models or philosophies lobbied strenuously for proposals and schemes that conformed to their vision of television. Each model found support inside the government and the ensuing debate engaged politicians, civil servants, the press and a host of organisations anxious about how the new medium would affect cultural, economic and political issues.

Given the challenging economic climate of the period is not surprising that throughout most of the 1950s the Department of Finance was opposed to *any* form of television coming to Ireland. Finance was mortified by the notion of the state taking on television as a public service given the immense costs associated with building studios and transmitters, purchasing the required equipment and hiring a large staff to operate TV. The cost of 'home produced' programmes was also a matter of great concern for the department. Finance was also convinced that the introduction of a privately owned commercial service which would not involve direct state expenditure would be problematic. It was worried about the prospect of consumers spending precious punts on what it defined as a 'luxury' and not putting their savings into Irish banks. Later when it became clear that television was inevitable, Finance insisted that a television service should only be established with the clear understanding that no cost should fall on the exchequer. In these circumstances, the department preferred to see a commercial service established that would be modelled on the Independent Television Authority in the United Kingdom or even the commercial networks in the United States.

The Department of Posts and Telegraphs, managed by the formidable Secretary, Leon Ó Broin, was already heavily involved in telecommunications, as it was responsible for the state's national radio service, Radio Éireann. The radio service, which had gone 'on the air' in 1926 was operated by civil servants in Posts and Telegraphs and was much maligned for what many regarded as the poor quality of its programming. It had been granted a nominal degree of independence in the early 1950s when Maurice Gorham was hired as Director and the Comhairle Radio Éireann was established to help supervise the service. In spite of this Radio Éireann remained under funded and in many respects, unpopular.[3]

As Secretary of Posts and Telegraphs, Leon Ó Broin played an important role in developing the structure of the national television service that emerged at the end of the decade. Ó Broin was a highly cultured man, a linguist who wrote history in his spare time and translated books from English into Irish for *An Gum*. Throughout the 1950s he relentlessly advocated the establishment of television as a 'public service' loosely based on the BBC. He maintained that it was imperative for cultural as well as political reasons that television be state owned and operated. The Department of Finance disagreed in the strongest of terms and these two departments engaged in frequent skirmishes when trying to influence governments throughout the decade. The structure of a future television service was the fundamental issue that had to be decided, as adoption of an independent commercial service or a government owned public service, would determine the content of programmes, the paramount issue of the debate. Posts and Telegraphs argued that a public service following the model of the BBC could be an important asset to the nation as it would broadcast educational and cultural programmes that would uplift and enlighten the citizen. Finance and its supporters, focused on economic development, believed that entrepreneurs should be encouraged to develop a service that would not impinge on scarce state resources. These two opposing concepts provided the terrain on which the television battle would be fought. This dialectical approach might seem somewhat superficial at first but the Irish television service that emerged in 1960 was a synthesis of these opposing ideas as it borrowed from both to produce what might be described as an Irish solution to an Irish problem.

Seán Lemass emerged as a key 'player' during this period both in his role as Minister for Industry and Commerce and Tánaiste and later as Taoiseach. Irish television is often times regarded as a product of Lemass's Ireland emerging in the 1960s as an agent that fostered cultural, social and political change. However, the reality is that television emerged out of the 1950s a period characterised by dire economic conditions. The decisions that were made about the structure of television in the state were informed by the crisis of the period. Joe Lee has pointed out that the 1956 census sent a shudder through Irish society and reverberated deep into the apparatus of the state. Simply put the country was in deep trouble. Emigration was bleeding the country white as 500,000 people had emigrated between the conclusion of the Second World War and 1960. The 1956 census was a shock, 'that convinced some key figures, most notable in Finance of the necessity for a fundamental change in direction. It was the closest Irish equivalent to the shame of surrender and occupation for continental countries in the Second World War.[4]

In this climate, as debates about television developed Lemass considered the commercial option as the best one for the government to adopt. He understood the arguments made by Ó Broin in favour of 'public service' television but did not see this as a practical or viable option. Lemass was also keenly aware of the proposals made by foreign corporations interested in developing a television service in Ireland and intrigued by the notion of a commercial network operating a national service and freeing the state from the burdensome task of building and operating this costly new medium. It is important to remember that Lemass was focused on economic development and convinced that every effort had to be made to revive the national economy. He was therefore sympathetic with the arguments put forward by the Department of Finance and concerned that underwriting a mammoth project like television would retard efforts to realise economic development.

As the department responsible for broadcasting matters, Posts and Telegraphs attracted numerous proposals and queries concerning television throughout the 1950s. Ó Broin was, therefore, well placed to influence government policy and keenly interested in trying to shape the structure and form of Irish television. In 1950, acting on his own initiative, Ó Broin set up a Television Committee within his department to investigate the new medium and how a native service might be developed. During this decade, under both Fianna Fáil and coalition governments, his department conducted studies and produced a number of reports that explored the options that were open to the state. He consulted with the BBC on a regular basis and corresponded regularly with the Director-General, Sir Ian Jacob. He found an important ally in the BBC which supported his efforts to establish Irish television as a public service.[5] Ó Broin considered the BBC as the best model for the Irish television to emulate, regarding the programmes broadcast by commercial networks in Britain and America with deep suspicion. Much to the consternation of Lemass and Finance he fully embraced the 'Rethian' philosophy of broadcasting.

While politicians, civil servants and interested citizens debated these issues television was making its way into homes along the eastern coast and in border areas. These broadcasts made their way into Ireland initially from Britain and later from Northern Ireland. By 1953 the BBC had built a temporary transmitter on Divis Mountain in Belfast which enabled people on both sides of the border to witness the coronation of Queen Elizabeth. Programmes routinely featured stories about the royal family and interviews with British and Unionist politicians. The Catholic Church complained about the 'immoral' element it detected in British programmes that were available as 'spillover' from Britain and Belfast. The inability of the state to offer an alternative created discomfort in Dublin and placed pressure on the state to come to a decision.

In 1957, while Neil Blaney was Minister for Posts and Telegraphs, Leon Ó Broin realised that the new Fianna Fáil Government was seriously considering offering a license to a private company to set up a commercial service. It is clear that one of the strongest voices behind this decision belonged to Lemass. An alarmed Ó Broin made a rushed and awkward effort to discredit the commercial option. His departmental television committee submitted a report to the cabinet, which challenged prevailing government policy and once again articulated the need for developing television as a 'public service'. The report argued that television was tremendously important but concluded that if the state could not afford to set up television as a public service it should simply not establish a native service. The report upset Lemass because the committee refused to consider seriously that a private commercial service might be the best alternative. While in the past, Ó Broin had tangled primarily with the Department of Finance, this report and Lemass's reaction to it ensured that the Tánaiste would stay involved in discussions centred on television policy. He was clearly disturbed with what he believed was as an ambiguous, incoherent document and expressed his concerns in a sharply worded letter to Neil Blaney. In this correspondence one can, for the first time, observe the future Taoiseach articulate his understanding of how government policy should prepare for television.

The Tánaiste was quick to take Blaney to task for what he regarded as an inferior effort on the part of his department. He complained, 'the Memorandum is unsatisfactory from many viewpoints. It is just the type of Memo which, as a member of the Government, I hate to get because it does not convey a clear picture of the problem and appears to be, in some respects, self-contradictory.'[6] He suggested a much more concise statement be made to the government, one that would not be the muddled, inconsistent submission that Posts and Telegraphs had produced. He told Blaney that the memo needed to be rewritten and that the issue should be put before the Cabinet in a clear fashion. 'I suggest that you should

put the TV issue to the Government in the following clear form: -
(1) A state TV service is ruled out on grounds of cost. (2) A TV
service must, therefore, be based on commercial advertising, and
be provided by private enterprise.'[7]

As far as he was concerned the Government had made a
decision, there was no need for additional debate. Lemass suggested that Blaney and his department outline for the Cabinet the
requirements that any prospective applicant would have to conform
to. 'My suggestion is that you should seek authority from the
Government to make a public announcement that proposals for a
commercial TV service be provided and operated by private enterprise will be considered subject to the following conditions: (1) No
cost to the Government. (2) Suitable machinery for the supervision
and control of programmes. (3) Free time for Public Services. (4)
Nation wide coverage. (5) Encouragement of the Irish language.'[8]

Lemass wanted the government to have the luxury of a concise
summary that would make a specific and coherent request. The
thirty-seven part, seventeen page document that he had reviewed
from the Department of Posts and Telegraphs was simply too
convoluted to enable the Cabinet to take decisive action. The
management strategy Lemass adopted in this instance would later
be employed when he became Taoiseach. Rather than be burdened
with a complex, contradictory submission that would confuse and
frustrate members of the Cabinet, Lemass wanted an explicit
memorandum that would recommend a clear option. The government then could debate the submission and come to a decision.

In concluding his letter to Blaney the Tánaiste suggested that,
once adequate guidelines had been established, the department
should quickly identify the one proposal that it thought was the
most suitable. Blaney was told that he should then request the
government's permission to make a commitment to the best
applicant. Lemass wanted a decision made by the government, and

a commitment given to a private commercial company that would allow a service to begin broadcasting. He certainly appreciated the argument that favoured a public service, but believed that the costs involved were beyond the state's resources. He saw no point in endless debate on the issue and was annoyed at the confusing memo produced by the Television Committee and Posts and Telegraphs. One can sense that Lemass had grown impatient and frustrated with both Blaney and Ó Broin. He believed commercial television provided a natural solution to the problem that confronted the Government, a solution that fit quite well with his philosophy of encouraging entrepreneurs and foreign investment.

However, he was unable to force the issue as amid these debates a Cabinet Committee was formed in October of 1957 to determine the most effective means of bringing television to Ireland. The establishment of the committee suggests Eamon de Valera's intervention, as the ageing Taoiseach always preferred the methodical approach to deciding difficult policy issues. The committee included Seán Lemass, the Minister for Posts and Telegraphs, Neil Blaney, the Minister for Finance, Dr James Ryan, and the Minister for External Affairs, Frank Aiken. This committee was established to examine television in light of the recent decisions that had been reached by the government. The new ministerial body was required to report to the government after exploring how an Irish television service could be introduced, 'as early as practicable, under public control . . . (and) . . . so far as possible . . . without cost to the Exchequer.'[9] Lemass dominated this short-lived committee and was certainly not afraid to seize the initiative in this committee nor was he hesitant to make important unilateral policy decisions.

The relationship between Posts and Telegraphs and Lemass's Cabinet Committee proved difficult as Ó Broin and his associates were on the receiving end of policy decisions they considered unacceptable. In the not so recent past the department had been a proactive one able to influence policy and debate regarding television. With the creation of the Cabinet Committee, the staff at Posts and Telegraphs found itself reacting to the committee's proposals and declarations. This new relationship was difficult for Ó Broin to accept. He was uncomfortable with the commercial direction that he believed Lemass and the Cabinet Committee were moving, and frustrated by his inability to convince the ministers to change their approach to television. The first task of the Cabinet Committee was to draft a public announcement that would be made by Neil Blaney, the Minister for Posts and Telegraphs. The Cabinet met in November of 1957 and decided that Blaney would issue a public statement inviting proposals from companies interested in television broadcasting in Ireland. This statement had been carefully drafted by Seán Lemass and approved by the Cabinet Committee. This was an important announcement as it provides an indication of what type of proposal Lemass and the government were looking for. It underscored the fact that a decision had been made to endorse the commercial option that would allow a private corporation to operate a television service.

Neil Blaney later addressed the Association of Advertisers in Ireland and revealed the government's new position on television. He announced that the government was:

> prepared to consider proposals from private interests for the provision of a transmission network that will ensure satisfactory reception in all parts of the country, as well as necessary studios and complementary indoor and outdoor equipment. The entire capital and maintenance costs will be met by the promoting group . . . in consideration of a license to operate commercial programmes for a term of years.[10]

Blaney revealed that his department had already received several very interesting proposals. Critically, he emphasised that it was anticipated that no cost would fall upon the Exchequer. He continued by outlining the structure of the Irish service and by defining its relationship with the state. 'The television system will become state property and will be under the control of a Television Authority. . . . The authority . . . will . . . make special arrangements regarding such matters as the presentation of news and the position of the Irish language. It will be a condition that part of the time will be made available for programmes of a public service character.'[11] Blaney also addressed the issue of advertisements, indicating that the government had decided to discard the ban on foreign commercials, a policy that had been in force on Radio Éireann since 1934. This provision fits with the emerging reality in Lemass's Ireland where competition would be encouraged and special or preferential treatment of Irish firms would be phased out. He acknowledged that to succeed commercial television would be heavily dependent on advertisements and that limiting access of non-native companies would be a mistake. The minister expressed confidence that Irish companies would still make, 'the maximum use of the new medium for advertising Irish goods to Irish people.'[12]

The November 1957 address, initiated by Lemass, marked a turning point in the painfully slow development of Irish television. The government made it clear that television in Ireland would be a service 'largely commercial in character' with 'private interests' responsible for building and running the service. The fact that the announcement was made at a convention of advertisers underscored the extent of the commercial commitment that was being made. The speech clearly reflected the desire of Lemass to grant a license to a private company, which would have an exclusive right to broadcast in Ireland.

If Ó Broin and the Television Committee were concerned with the decisions that the Cabinet Committee had made, a letter from the Department of Industry and Commerce in December 1957

caused genuine alarm. This concerned two proposals that had
been submitted to and rejected by the government earlier in the
year. One of the firms was the Texas based McLendon Corporation.
The American proposal offered what amounted to a free television
service for the country if the company was granted permission to
set up a commercial radio service that could broadcast into Britain.
A similar proposal was made by a Paris-based company owned and
operated by a Romanian exile, Charles Michelson. The price would
be rather steep as these proposals would require the Irish government to withdraw from the Copenhagen Agreement, a treaty signed
by the state, which governed the use on international wavelengths.
In spite of this Lemass regarded each as attractive schemes, which
deserved close consideration outside of the Cabinet Committee.
This signalled a new departure and an abrupt change because
Lemass believed that the Michelson scheme could help promote
the economic growth he was so desperate to cultivate. Michelson
had spent considerable time in Ireland and tailored his proposal to
the government's needs. The Romanian ex-patriot met with the
heads of a number of semi-state boards and offered each free access
to the commercial radio service that he wanted to build in Ireland.
Lemass told Ó Broin that a decision had been made 'in favour of a
combination of sound broadcasting and television on the basis
which would meet the representations of Bord Fáilte Éireann, Aer
Lingus, and Hospital Trust.'[13] A short time later Lemass informed
the new Minister for Posts and Telegraphs, Seán Ormonde,[14] that
the Cabinet Committee had made a number of decisions about the
direction television should take. He sent the Cabinet Committee's
conclusions to Ormonde, and ordered Posts and Telegraphs to
redraft the document into a formal memo that would be submitted
to the government for a decision. Posts and Telegraphs was instructed to review all the proposals that had been submitted and to
report back to the Cabinet Committee recommending the one

company that best conformed to conditions that had been outlined by Lemass and his associates.[15]

Ormonde responded with a document that was highly critical of the decisions made by the Cabinet Committee. The response, written by Leon Ó Broin but supported by Ormonde was clearly intended for Lemass, as it contained a robust critique of the Cabinet Committee's decision. It is clear that Ó Broin believed the Cabinet Committee's decision to reverse established government policy, concerning the Michelson and McLendon proposals, signalled a disastrous shift that would have terrible consequences for the country. Ó Broin expressed his disappointment with the Cabinet Committee complaining that he was 'profoundly unhappy' with the conclusion that it come to. He maintained that the decisions violated every feature of the policy that the Television Committee had developed since its inception in 1950. Ó Broin warned that if television was organised along the lines that the Cabinet Committee had suggested the government would experience 'constant trouble'.[16] Lemass responded to the Posts and Telegraphs memoranda quickly. He had hoped that the department would act on the Cabinet Committee's submission and prepare the memorandum he wanted to submit to the full Cabinet. In his response one can sense a growing impatience with both Ó Broin and Ormonde. The Tánaiste tersely stated that the Cabinet Committee had envisioned a commercial monopoly in their report and dismissed Ó Broin's efforts to find an alternative.

> It has been accepted that a TV service must be provided on a commercial basis and while, like Mr Ó Broin, most of us would prefer a public service if this were possible, it is, as you know, out of the question for financial reasons. The Government have decided to proceed on the basis of a commercial service and this question must be regarded as settled.[17]

Lemass stated that he wanted Posts and Telegraphs to comply with the wishes of the Cabinet Committee and draft a submission to the government that would embrace the report his committee had issued. In responding to Ó Broin's polemic against McLendon and Michelson, the Tánaiste stated that the Cabinet Committee was aware of the complications that would be involved if one of these proposals was accepted. He maintained that although no decision had been reached the Cabinet Committee 'clearly understood that accepting either of these proposals would require Ireland to withdraw from the Copenhagen Agreement'.

Posts and Telegraphs complied with the wishes of Lemass and prepared a formal submission to the government, which endorsed the report of the Cabinet Committee. Seán Ormonde accepted Lemass's offer to submit the views of his department with the formal submission for the government. The formal document set out the procedure that would allow for a selection of what was described as a 'concessionaire'. Once the government had set the conditions of the contract that would be employed, Posts and Telegraphs would be responsible for nominating the candidate that best conformed to the conditions outlined by the Cabinet Committee. At this juncture it appeared that the wishes of Lemass and his Cabinet Committee would prevail and that momentum was building towards the establishment of a privately owned commercial service.

However at the last minute the efforts of Lemass were frustrated by a suggestion submitted by the Minister of Health. Seán MacEntee, Lemass's long time nemesis, suggested that the government should consider the procedure that was put in place in 1925 when an official government commission was established to consider how radio should be established in the state. His proposal to establish a television commission was quickly accepted by the government. Lemass had shown a desire to get a service 'on the air' quickly, and had illustrated a determination to take the difficult decisions to achieve this end. However, once MacEntee's proposal had been circulated, it became difficult to justify opposition to the concept of an official commission that would review all proposals received by the state and provide a recommendation to the government. The decision to accept MacEntee's proposal suggests once again the influence of the Taoiseach, Eamon de Valera. It also highlights the limits of Lemass's influence in the last Government of the elderly Taoiseach. De Valera's exhaustive, methodical style of management was in sharp contrast to the more determined Lemass who in a very short amount of time had immersed himself deeply in the government's evolving television policy. Although this may have been a tactical defeat for Lemass he showed no interest in abandoning his opposition to 'public service' television and continued to be active in influencing the governments television policy.

The government announced in March 1958 that a Television Commission would be established by the Minister of Posts and Telegraphs to examine all aspects of television broadcasting and to make recommendations to the government. The fact that Posts and Telegraphs would oversee the work of the commission insured that Ó Broin would remain closely involved in the state's emerging television policy. Ó Broin and his staff worked closely with the Television Commission, and used every opportunity to try and influence the findings of this body. Posts and Telegraphs would also have to work with Lemass who limited the scope of the Commission by personally writing its terms of reference. These terms had profound implications for the commission and certainly limited the scope and effectiveness of its work. Lemass drafted instructions, which were both concise and supported by Finance and the Taoiseach. Unlike the terms proposed by Ó Broin, the Tánaiste wanted the commission's work to be strictly defined when the question of financing television was concerned. He proposed that the Television Commission be created with instructions that would specify, 'that no charge should fall on the Exchequer, on capital or current account.'[18] This effectively eliminated the public service model from consideration.

This was the most critical qualification inserted into the commission's orders. This stipulation succeeded in limiting the ability of the Television Commission to conduct a thorough investigation and precluded it from submitting a truly comprehensive report to the government. It is clear that the Tánaiste was not interested in dredging up the subject of public service television, or the model advocated by the Television Committee. He clearly believed that such a proposal was out of the question given the financial difficulties that the state was experiencing. Lemass contended that the commission should investigate all the proposals that had been received by Posts and Telegraphs and make a recommendation as to which scheme should be accepted by the government. The terms of reference conformed to the proposal that had been made by Lemass and clearly supported the thinking of the Tánaiste and the Department of Finance.[19] The terms also proved that the government did not want to ignore any proposals that had been submitted to the government. It wanted the commission to evaluate closely all submissions received by the Post Office including those made by Michelson and McLendon.

The commission heard evidence from a wide range of groups, and sorted through proposals from domestic and foreign companies interested in gaining an exclusive licence to set up a television station in Ireland. Many of the proposals were from foreign companies, some with subsidiaries in Ireland, though Gael Linn submitted one of the more informed and comprehensive applications. The Gael Linn application made it clear that it viewed television as a tool to revive the Irish language. Gordon McLendon, outfitted in cowboy boots and a ten-gallon hat appeared before the commission to make the case that his company's proposal was an opportunity that was simply too good to be turned down. Charles Michelson spent weeks in Ireland meeting with politicians and businessmen trying to line up support for his scheme. The result was that his firm received support from a number of semi-state companies and intriguingly also from the Vatican. Lemass was intrigued by the Michelson proposal in spite of the difficulties inherent in the scheme. Michelson offered to provide a two channel national service at no cost to the state. But there would of course be a price and this came in the form of a license to broadcast a commercial radio station from Irish territory into Britain. This would require the Government to withdraw from the Copenhagen agreement which Ireland was a signatory to and which allocated wavelengths throughout Europe. The agreement restricted the use of wavelengths and made both the McLendon and Michelson proposals unfeasible.

Leon Ó Broin appeared before the Commission to voice his opposition to the commercial option. Using the wealth of technical and financial information from the various proposals that had come into his department he offered an alternative. This proposed the state fund and operate a service that would generate revenue by selling 'air time' to advertisers. He also hoped to convince the BBC to offer programmes to the Irish service at greatly reduced rates. He was convinced this compromise could work and believed that popular commercial programmes could generate revenue while educational programmes could balance the commercial component. Importantly the state would maintain control of the medium and not turn it over to a private entrepreneur simply motivated by a desire to realise a profit.

The Television Commission submitted its report to the government in May of 1959. The document was a confusing, contradictory report that failed to reach any real consensus, or present a coherent recommendation to the government. Parts of the document were well researched and provided a great deal of information concerning how television might contribute to Irish society. However, in the final analysis the report was a disappointing effort. The failure of the commission can be traced directly to the terms of reference, which limited the scope and depth of its investigation.

At this juncture and possibly seeing an opening Posts and Telegraphs submitted a revised proposal to the government that appeared much more attractive in light of the confused and contradictory report issued by the Television Commission. There can be little doubt that the three companies that the Television Commission had 'short listed' failed to impress Seán Lemass and other members of the Cabinet including the Minister for Finance. Ó Broin and his associates were able to put together a more detailed proposal that requested financial support from the state, but also promised a return on the government's investment. The proposal indicated that by accepting the principle that no *ultimate* charge should fall on the Exchequer, a state-owned service could be up and running quickly. Post and Telegraphs argued that this state-run service would be able to make a profit and pay back the loan that would allow it to get 'on the air'. The Department of Finance reluctantly acknowledged that it would support a service along the lines that had been outlined by Posts and Telegraphs. Debates in the Dáil illustrate that deputies realised that the Television Commission's Report was not an enthusiastic endorsement of a private commercial service. At this juncture Ó Broin was perfectly positioned to try to persuade the government that a change in policy had to be made.

Lemass became Taoiseach in June of 1959. A short time later met with and Ó Broin, to discuss television. In this meeting the Secretary for Posts and Telegraphs was able to put his case before the new Taoiseach. In his autobiography, Ó Broin maintains that the change of policy endorsed by the government was due to Lemass:

> can only surmise as to how the government's final decision was arrived at. Seán Lemass, who a couple of months before had taken over as Taoiseach from de Valera, had no doubt a lot to do with it. He asked me to go and see him. The interview was brief. I was concerned, I told him, about the quality of programmes. We were fortunately placed in close proximity to what was probably the best service in the world, the BBC, an entirely public service organisation, and I suggested that we might explore the possibility of a special arrangement for an extension of their service as a back-up to such programmes of quality that we could produce at home on a similar public service basis. He made no comment, but as I spoke of the BBC I felt that the chauvinists among us would not take too well to any arrangements with the *British* Broadcasting Corporation.[20]

Ó Broin, who had believed that the BBC could be a valuable part of an Irish public service, recognised at this juncture that this would be very difficult for political reasons. However this did not preclude the government from considering the Post Office plan *sans* BBC involvement. The government's ultimate decision surprised Ó Broin who described the announcement that was made in July of 1959 as:

> An extraordinary *volte face* occurred. The government, again without consultation with us, but obviously returning to our television committee's reports, rejected the view of the commission and proceeded to set up a statutory authority to run both television and radio without any commercial promoters whatever.'[21]

John Horgan has pointed out that other pressures were brought to bear on the Taoiseach, pointing to his 1969 interview with Michael Mills of the *Irish Press*.[22] In the interview Lemass explained that he was not in favour of setting up television as a semi-state body, 'I was in favour at that stage of giving it over to one of the private groups who were seeking the service. There was Gael Linn and another Irish group and a number of foreign groups were interested in the service. But the government decided it should be a State service.' This statement suggests that once again Lemass ran into trouble at the Cabinet level on the question of the structure of television, but this time not as Tánaiste but as Taoiseach. In the end the Lemass Government came to a final decision at a Cabinet meeting on 31 July 1959.[23] A good deal of credit for keeping the medium out of the hands of private enterprise could be claimed by Ó Broin. He was successful in his persistent efforts to convince the government to accept the principle of a state-owned and operated public television service that would look to revenue from advertisers to sustain itself.

At the first meeting of the RTÉ Authority in June of 1960 the new Minster for Posts and Telegraphs, Michael Hilliard, delivered an address which had been written, reviewed and edited by the Taoiseach, who remained engaged in television and concerned with its cost. Hilliard made it clear that there were important matters that he wanted to share privately with the new Authority. It is revealing to note that the first issue on the Minister's agenda concerned the finances of the new service. This was unambiguously linked to the Authority's independence from the government. The Minister explained that the government believed that television should be 'self-supporting within a reasonable period'. He emphasised that this was 'a fundamental matter so far as the well-being of your organisation is concerned. Genuine independence may be a matter of outlook but it is, unfortunately, as often a matter of finances'.[24]

The new Authority had been put on notice that the financial stability of the new service was imperative and that any serious difficulty in this regard would place the independence of Telefís Éireann at risk. The Authority was promised that it was the government's intention to give the new organisation 'the greatest possible freedom from direct State control', but warned that as long as state funding was involved 'there will remain a temptation – and I will put it no stronger – for the state to interfere in matters which will be properly your concern.'[25] It is important to point out that the issue of financial stability was one that was critical to the Lemass government. The fear that had been expressed by the Department of Finance about television becoming a drain of the national exchequer remained a real concern for the state. The government's insistence that Telefís Éireann generate substantial income quickly influenced the character and ultimately the programmes transmitted by the fledgling service.

Although the new service was not scheduled to go 'on the air' until 1961, Lemass was concerned with the impact the new medium would have on Irish society. Like his predecessor, Eamon de Valera, the Taoiseach was uneasy with the advent of Irish television. Both men believed that the state should have a strong voice in determining what should and should not be broadcast on an Irish service. Lemass and de Valera argued that it was essential that the government protect the Irish people from what both considered the potentially insidious influence an unsupervised service might impart.[26] The concern of Lemass is evident in the strict instructions he wrote for the television authority his government had recently appointed. The Taoiseach was clearly interested in trying to influence the authority, as can be seen by his decision to issue what he termed 'policy directives'. Lemass drafted these instructions a few months before the television authority was scheduled to convene for its inaugural session. In a detailed memorandum to the secretary of his department, Maurice Moynihan, Lemass stated that he felt it was imperative the authority understands that 'stage-Irishisms (and) playboyisms' should be avoided. Instead he argued that the station should produce an 'image' of a vigorous progressive nation, seeking efficiency'.[27] In regards to social and economic problems that challenged the country he emphasised that television should 'encourage objective presentation of facts and constructive comment. The "God-help-us" approach should be ruled out'.[28]

Although he believed television could be used in an intelligent manner, he cautioned:

> objectivity should not be allowed to excuse the undue representation of our faults. What you should aim to present is a picture of Ireland and the Irish as we would like to have it, although our hopes and aims may well be helped by the objective presentation of facts in association with constructive comment.[29]

He made it clear that Irish television needed to avoid coverage or comment about Northern Ireland that might upset the Stormont Government, and maintained that the issue of partition should be addressed only with the greatest of care. According to the Taoiseach, the new authority had to act with prudence when dealing with other sensitive topics such as sex, religion, and education.

Lemass's memo met with resistance from the secretary of his department, who argued that the 'policy directives' were unnecessarily severe and would ultimately prove counter-productive. In a courageous memorandum, Maurice Moynihan tried to dissuade the Taoiseach from issuing orders he considered draconian. He argued that the recently passed broadcasting act made provision for the Taoiseach's concerns by establishing a strong, government appointed, public authority charged with overseeing Irish television. Moynihan argued that dictating terms to this new organisation would be seen, 'both at home and abroad, as an illiberal action, calculated to hamper unduly the freedom of the Broadcasting Authority.'[30] The secretary also pointed out that the proposed directives ran counter to the spirit of Article 40 of the Irish Constitution that 'guarantees liberty of expression for organs of public opinion'.[31]

In spite of Moynihan's best efforts, Lemass insisted that the 'policy directives' be issued, as he believed they would provide important guidelines for the authority. To underscore this concern he ordered that the written directives be incorporated into a formal speech that would be delivered by the Minister of Posts and Telegraphs at the inaugural meeting of the board. He insisted that printed copies of the directives be distributed to each member of the Authority in order to ensure that that all were aware of the government's position. Lemass rejected Moynihan's assertion that through the appointed Authority the government would have the final word on television, declaring, 'On these matters it is not enough to have the last word, if we do not have the first.'[32]

Lemass would one day claim that Irish television was 'an instrument of public policy'. One could make the case that this, perhaps his most famous statement about Irish television, had its roots in these policy directives. His relationship with the new television service proved a fractious one throughout his tenure as Taoiseach.

Conclusion

Seán Lemass stepped down as Taoiseach in 1966 and was replaced by Jack Lynch. He remained a Dáil Deputy until 1969, when he retired from active politics. Lemass died on 11 May 1971, a victim, it would appear, to the omnipresent pipe he enjoyed so much. Ironically, Eamon de Valera, whom he had succeeded as Taoiseach in 1959, outlived Lemass by four years. By this time Lemass's own reputation as one of the most significant figures of twentieth-century Ireland was well established.

In many ways Lemass deserves his reputation as the great Irish moderniser. Seán Lemass was not a radical reformer but an astute politician who learned to adapt to survive. Nevertheless, he was the single individual most responsible for leading the country out from the confines of economic nationalism that retarded economic progress in independent Ireland. Indeed, it is one of the many paradoxes of Irish history that Lemass, as minister in earlier Fianna Fáil governments, was the architect of the very protectionist policy that he later abolished. By time he became Taoiseach Lemass was an experienced and confident political leader. He was also convinced that Ireland's future lay in moving away from the suffocating insularity that had characterised the new state since its foundation.

The policies initiated by Lemass were supported by the world-wide economic growth that took place during his tenure as Taoiseach and marked a clear departure for Ireland. Lemass encouraged foreign investment and the development of an export-oriented economy that would ultimately take advantage of a common European market. Although he failed to secure Ireland's entry into the EEC, he clearly believed that the country's future depended on developing closer social and economic ties with the continent. One hundred years after his birth, Seán Lemass's legacy became visible in the Ireland of the 'Celtic Tiger'. His desire to see Ireland emerge as a self confident European nation, providing attractive opportunities for its citizens had been realised before the economy imploded. Although the economy collapsed and emigration has once again become a part of Irish life, the economic growth of the 1990s that continued into the new millennium transformed Ireland. Although prosperity brought with it many social problems, Ireland is no longer concerned about its viability as a state. It should be remembered that when Lemass first became Taoiseach there was real debate as to whether or not Ireland had a future. Tremendous challenges confronted Lemass and his generation of political leaders. High rates of emigration in the post-war period underscored the native government's failure to provide for its citizens. With the support of a talented and equally courageous team of civil servants, most notably Dr Thomas Kenneth Whitaker, the Secretary of the Department of Finance, Lemass began the process of turning Ireland around. He was responsible for reorienting the nation, moving away from the Sinn Féin ethos of self sufficiency to a more broadminded economic and political philosophy that recognised that Ireland's future was dependent on fully engaging with a wider world.

Economic initiatives aside, Lemass will be remembered for instigating policies that to this day influence the direction of Irish society. As Taoiseach, Lemass made a genuine effort to improve relations with both London and Belfast. The British reciprocated his efforts and were anxious to encourage Lemass's desire to develop a close working relationship with London and a dialogue with Unionist in Belfast. Lemass's efforts to obtain a public commitment from the British government stipulating that London would not stand in the way of reunification were without success in the 1960s. However, this position was eventually accepted by London and endorsed in the failed Sunningdale Agreement of 1971, the Anglo-Irish Agreement of 1985, and the Good Friday Agreement of 1998. Lemass identified the attainment of such a commitment as an important goal of his government as early as 1960, believing it would be a critical step in addressing the problem of partition. Lemass demonstrated the courage and conviction to try to make progress where little had been made before. In this regard he laid the foundation upon which his successors would build.

As a veteran of the Easter Rising, the War of Independence and the Civil War, and as one who lost a brother to political violence, Lemass was uniquely positioned to begin the process of moving his party and his country out from the narrow political confines that had limited his predecessors. His desire to engage the government of Northern Ireland was a sincere effort to find common ground where both administrations could at least begin a dialogue. The concept of economic co-operation as a way to encourage reunification was overly optimistic, even simplistic. Nevertheless it was a genuine attempt to try and find an alternative to non-recognition and a departure from the hostility that had defined relations between Dublin and Belfast since the Government of Ireland Act partitioned the island in 1920. Although rebuffed by Lord Brookeborough, a more receptive Prime Minister, Terence O'Neill, responded to Lemass's overtures. Unfortunately, by the time a dialogue developed at the prime ministerial level, events closer to the ground were quickly moving in another, more depressing direction. The civil rights movement, the reaction it provoked from the less moderate Unionist community, and the emergence of the Provisional IRA insured that compromise would be much more difficult.

Although he might deny it publically, Seán Lemass had an uneasy relationship with the Irish Catholic Church. He was, in many respects, 'in the trenches' during long and very difficult encounters with the church and especially with the Archbishop of Dublin, John Charles McQuaid. Although he knew that the government had to move carefully on issues that concerned the church, he understood that the 'modern Ireland' he envisioned needed to be less Catholic in its constitution. He realised that a more distinct line had to be drawn between church and state. As a confident elder statesman, before retiring as Taoiseach, he established a constitutional committee to explore a number of thorny issues, including how state could be more inclusive in recognising the sensibilities of Protestants throughout the island. The Constitutional Committee, in which he himself participated, recommended that de Valera's 1937 Constitution be amended in this regard. It is important to recognise that this committee initiated a debate that instigated a wider discussion about other sensitive issues, such as divorce, contraception and abortion, in more recent decades.

Although often described as Ireland's 'great moderniser', when dealing with the emerging television service, Lemass's attitude towards modernisation proved quite ambivalent; the accelerating modernity he did so much to encourage proved a two-edged sword. Television changed the political culture of the country, becoming a popular and tenacious critic of the status quo. As Taoiseach he found himself in the uncomfortable position of being on the defensive, answerable to an increasingly aggressive and often hostile press. These changes were rapid and for many disorienting, proving that television was a critical agent of Ireland's transformation during the 1960s. His efforts to control the broadcast media and shape or spin its output proved futile.

As this short book argues, Lemass could be ambivalent about how to move forward on a number of difficult issues. His apprenticeship under de Valera was inordinately long and must have been frustrating. When he took over from 'the Chief', he moved deliberately and methodically to modernise Irish society. Lemass was first and foremost a successful politician who, when given the chance, carefully took full advantage of opportunities that were presented to him. The Lemass years in government represented a very real watershed in the history of modern Ireland. The choices he made and the course he set for his country have profoundly influenced Irish politics and society.

Notes

Introduction

1 Lemass interview with Michael Mills, *Irish Press*, 20 January 1969.

2 C. S. Andrews, *Man of No Property* (Cork, 1982), pp 23–4.

3 Quoted in John Horgan, *Seán Lemass: The Enigmatic Patriot* (Dublin, 1991), p. 29.

4 Brian Farrell, *Seán Lemass* (Dublin, 1991), p. 17.

5 Andrews, *Man of No Property*. Andrews maintains that Lemass was the architect of the 'New Departure' within Sinn Féin, which argued that the party had to 'concentrate on politically realizable objectives'.

6 Quoted in Farrell, *Lemass*, p. 17.

7 For a detailed critique of the Evans book see Brian Girvin's review published in *Reviews in History* (review no. 1447 www.history.ac.uk/reviews/review/1447, date accessed: 6 Oct., 2014). The author's response is included on the *Reviews in History* website.

Chapter 1: *Seán Lemass and the Politics of Economic Policy*

1 Memorandum from Lemass to Moynihan, 21 November 1944, quoted in John Horgan, *Seán Lemass: The Enigmatic Patriot* (Dublin, 1991), p. 114.

2 'The Ireland that we dreamed of' radio broadcast, 17 March 1943, in *Speeches and Statements of Eamon de Valera*, ed., Maurice Moynihan (Dublin, 1980), pp. 466–9.

3 Paul Bew and Henry Patterson, *Seán Lemass and the Making of Modern Ireland* (Dublin, 1982), p. 5.

4 Horgan, *Lemass*, p. 115.

5 Record of a meeting between Lemass and the British Prime Minister, 12 July 1959, (PRO, FO 1011/214).

6 Bew and Patterson, *Seán Lemass and the Making of Modern Ireland*, p. 3.

7 J. J. Lee, *Ireland 1912–1985: Politics and Society* (Cambridge, 1989), p. 188.

8 Ibid., p. 191.

9 Cormac Ó Grada, *A Rocky Road: The Irish Economy since the 1920s* (Manchester, 1997), p. 108.

10 L. M. Cullen, *An Economic History of Ireland since 1660* (London, 1987), p. 178.

11 Ronan Fanning, *Independent Ireland* (Dublin, 1983), p. 148.

12 See especially John Horgan's biography.

13 See Fanning, *Independent Ireland*, p. 149.

14 See Richard Dunphy, *The Making of Fianna Fáil Power in Ireland, 1923–1948* (Oxford, 1995). Dunphy notes that Lemass's proposal concerning unemployment did not receive support from the Taoiseach but was met with 'the usual de Valera fudge', p. 229.

15 Ibid., p. 238.

16 Ibid., p. 244.

17 See Bew and Patterson, *Lemass and the Making of Modern Ireland*, pp 31–2.

18 Dunphy, *The Making of Fianna Fáil Power*, p. 247.

19 J. J. Lee, 'Squaring the economic and social circles', in Philip Hannon and Jackie Gallagher, eds, *Taking the Long View: 70 Years of Fianna Fáil* (Dublin, 1996), p. 58.

20 See Ó Grada, *A Rocky Road*, p. 110.

21 Bew and Patterson, *Lemass and the Making of Modern Ireland*, p. 59.

22 Ó Grada, *A Rocky Road*, p. 27.

23 Although anaemic economy created tremendous social problems, the stereotype of Ireland as a cultural wasteland has been challenged recently most notably by Brian Fallon in *An Age of Innocence: Irish Culture 1930–1960* (Dublin, 1998).

24 Speech by Seán Lemass, 12 February 1952 (NAI, GIS 1/212).

25 Cited in Ó Grada, *A Rocky Road*, p. 112.

26 Minutes of meeting between Lemass and a deputation from the Association of the Chamber of Commerce of Ireland, 10 October 1952 (NAI TIC 32682).

27 Ibid., Speech by Lemass, 16 October 1952.

28 Ibid.

29 Lemass, interview with Michael Mills, *Irish Press*, 27 January 1969.

30 Speech by Lemass, 30 March 1957, NAI, GS 1/215.

31 Brian Farrell, *Seán Lemass* (Dublin, 1991), p. 93.

32 Lee, *Ireland 1922–1985*, p. 373.

33 Fanning, *Independent Ireland*, p. 191. See also Brendan M. Walsh, 'Economic growth and development 1945–70, in Lee, ed., *Ireland 1945–1970* (Dublin, 1979).

34 *Irish Times*, 18 January 1957.

35 Ibid.

36 Speech by Lemass, University College, Dublin, 5 December 1958 (NAI, GS 1/215).

37 Ibid.

38 Lee, 'Squaring the economic and social circles', in *Taking the Long View*, p. 59.

39 Speech by Lemass, University College Dublin, 5 December 1958 (NAI, GS 1/215).

40 Ibid.

41 Lee, *Ireland 1912–1985*, p. 359.

42 Terence Brown, *Ireland a Social and Cultural History, 1922 to the Present* (London, 1985) p. 185.

43 The economic historian Cormac Ó Grada has pointed out that a number of factors may have contributed to the sustained economic growth that developed from the late 1950s – including the boost in public confidence when Lemass replaced the ageing de Valera, combined with a commitment of Ireland's trading partners to trade liberalisation. See Ó Grada, *A Rocky Road*, p. 29.

Chapter 2: *Lemass and Northern Ireland*

1 Jonathan Bardon, *A History of Ulster* (Belfast, 1994), p. 629.

2 J. J. Lee, *Ireland 1912–1985: Politics and Society* (Cambridge, 1989), p. 367.

3 Brian Farrell, *Seán Lemass* (Dublin, 1991), p. 114.

4 John Horgan, *Seán Lemass: The Enigmatic Patriot* (Dublin, 1991), p. 287.

5 J. M. Skelly, *Irish Diplomacy at the United Nations, 1945–65; National Interests and International Order* (Dublin, 1997), p. 22.

6 *Irish Times*, 18 May 1949, quoted in Paul Bew and Henry Patterson, *Seán Lemass and the Making of Modern Ireland* (Dublin, 1982), p. 11.

7 Memorandum by Lemass, 4 September 1959 (NAI, S936 I/694).

8 See Chapter 3.

9 Quoted in Horgan, *Lemass*, p. 170.

10 Address by Lemass to the American League for an Undivided Ireland, New York, 6 October 1953 (NAI, GIS 1/213, p. 1).

11 Ibid., p. 2.

12 Ibid.

13 Ibid., p. 3.

14 Address by Lemass to the National Press Club, Washington DC, 1 October 1953 (ibid.).

15 Address by Lemass to the Ottawa Canadian Club, Ottawa, 25 September 1953 (ibid.).

16 *Belfast Telegraph*, 9 July 1959.

17 Ibid.

18 *Irish Times*, 6 July 1959.

19 Ibid.

20 *Dáil Debates*, cxxxvi, 1576–7 (21 July 1959).

21 *Irish Press*, 22 March 1961.

22 One of Brookeborough's most notorious speeches, delivered in July 1933, advised employees to hire only Protestants, indicating 'he had not a Roman Catholic about his own place' and warned that 'Roman Catholics were endeavoring to get in everywhere'. Quoted in Michael Farrell, *The Orange State* (London, 1980), p. 90.

23 Gibson to Brookeborough, 14 July 1951 (PRONI, CAB 9A/30/9).

24 Ibid.

25 Brookeborough to Gibson, 28 June 1951 (ibid.).

26 In 1932 he warned that the failure to halt the infiltration of Catholics would 'result in their becoming in a few years so numerous that they would be able to vote Ulster into the Free State', see Bardon, *Ulster*, p. 538.

27 Brookeborough to Gibson, 28 June 1951 (PRONI, CAB 9A/30/9).

28 Memo from Con Cremin, Department of External Affairs, to Department of Taoiseach, 5 October 1959, (NAI, S936 I/694).

29 Ibid.

30 *Hansard*, NI Commons, xxxxv: 230 (221 October 1959).

31 Ibid.

32 Cabinet Conclusions, 19 March 1959 (PRONI, CAB 4/1085).

33 Ibid.

34 Ibid.

35 Ibid.

36 Ibid.

37 Cabinet Conclusions, 9 July 1959 (ibid.).

38 See Michael Kennedy, 'Towards co-operation: Seán Lemass and north-south economic relations, 1956–65', *Irish Economic and Social History*, xxiv (1997).

39 *Irish Press*, 5 September 1959.

40 Oxford Union speech, 15 October 1959 (NAI, S936I/694).

41 Ibid.

42 Ibid.

43 Ibid., quoted in Lee, *Ireland 1912–1985*, p. 368.

44 This issue was discussed between Lemass and Macmillan in a meeting at Downing Street in March 1963; see PRO, PREM 11/4320.

45 Horgan, *Lemass*, p. 257.

46 Quoted in Lee, *Ireland 1912–1985*, p. 369.

47 Speech by Lemass at Manhattan Hotel, Tralee, 29 July 1963 (NAI, S16272 D/95).

48 Ibid.

49 Leon Ó Broin, *Just Like Yesterday* (Dublin, 1985), p. 211.

50 Lynch to Lemass, 16 March 1966 (NAI 96/6/23). Aiken preferred 'the Six Counties of Northern Ireland'.

51 Lemass to Lynch, 18 March 1966 (ibid.). Two years later when the Prime Minister of Northern Ireland, Terence O'Neill, visited the new Taoiseach, Jack Lynch, he specifically requested that the terms 'Northern Ireland' and 'Northern Ireland Government' be adopted 'in all publicity, including radio and television' (memo of O'Neill–Lynch meeting, Dublin, 8 January 1968, ibid.).

52 Blythe to Lemass, 28 November 1962 (NAI, S16272D).

53 Ibid.

54 Quoted in Horgan, *Lemass*, p. 263.

55 Lemass to Blythe, 7 December 1962 (NAI, S16272D).

56 Ibid.

57 Ibid.

58 Marc Mulholland, *Terence O'Neill* (Dublin, 2013), p. 38.

59 Ibid., p. 87.

60 Memo from O'Neill to Douglas-Home, 22 November 1963 (PRO, PREM 4964).

61 Ibid.

62 Ibid.

63 Ibid.

64 'Note for the Record', minutes of a meeting between O'Neill and Douglas-Home (ibid.).

65 Terence O'Neill, *Autobiography* (London, 1972), p. 53.

66 *Belfast Telegraph*, 18 March 1964

67 *Irish Times*, 28 March 1964.

68 Memo, 11 November 1963 (NAI, S16272 F/95).

69 *Irish Times*, 31 January 1964.

70 Ibid.

71 *Irish Press*, 15 February 1964.

72 Childers to Lemass, 7 October 1964 (NAI, S16272 F/95).

73 Ibid.

74 Ibid.

75 Lemass to Childers, 8 October 1964 (ibid.).

76 O'Neill, *Autobiography*, p. 68.

77 Lemass interview with Michael Mills, *Irish Press*, 28 January 1969.

78 Ibid.

Chapter 3: *Lemass and the British*

1 Lemass interview, *Irish Independent*, 4 April 1965.

2 Kimber to Chadwick, Colonial Office, 10 February 1959 (PRO, DO 35/7906).

3 Ibid.

4 See Robert Fisk, *In Time of War, Ireland, Ulster and the Price of Neutrality, 1939–45* (London, 1983), p. 309.

5 Kimber to Chadwick, 10 February 1959 (PRO, DO 35/7906).

6 Ibid.

7 Clutterbuck to Lord Home, 20 August 1959 (ibid., DO 35/10772).

8 Quoted in John Horgan, *Seán Lemass: The Enigmatic Patriot* (Dublin, 1991), pp. 253–4.

9 Memo, June 1959 (PRO, DO 35/7906).

10 Memo from Laithwaite to Home, 3 July 1959 (ibid.).

11 Ibid.

12 Personality report on Lemass for Macmillan, 1959 (PRO, PREM 11/4320).

13 Ibid.

14 Record of a Lemass–Macmillan meeting, 13 July 1959 (PRO, PREM 1011/214).

15 Ibid.

16 Ibid.

17 Ibid.

18 David Anderson, British Embassy, Dublin, to O. R. Blair, Commonwealth Office, London, 7 June 1960 (ibid., DO 35/7824).

19 Telegram to Commonwealth Office from Dublin, 31 January 1963 (ibid., PREM 11/4320).

20 Ibid.

21 Record of a meeting at Admiralty House, 18 March 1963 (ibid.).

22 Ibid.

23 Ibid.

24 Ibid.

25 Briefing document for the Prime Minister, 13 May 1964 (ibid.).

26 Ibid.

27 Ibid.

28 Record of a conversation between British and Irish Prime Ministers, 18 March 1964 (ibid.).

29 Lemass interview, *Irish Independent*, 23 April 1965.

30 Wilson to Lemass, 22 February 1965 (NAI, 96/6/778).

31 Ibid.

32 Memo, Department of the Taoiseach, 22 February 1965 (ibid.).

33 Lemass interview with Mills, *Irish Press*, 29 January 1969.

Chapter 4: *Lemass and the Catholic Church*

1 *Irish Independent*, 14 March 1925, quoted in J. J. Lee, *Ireland 1912–1985: Politics and Society* (Cambridge, 1989), pp 160–1.

2 Lemass to Byrne, 8 July 1927 (DDA, Abp Byrne Papers).

3 Ibid.

4 Ibid.

5 Archbishop's Office to Lemass, 13 July 1927 (ibid.).

6 Lemass to Rev. Patrick Dunne, 19 July 1927 (ibid.).

7 Thanks to archivist David Sheehy, Dublin Diocesan Archives for this information.

8 References to the 'church' and the 'hierarchy' in this chapter refer to the Catholic Church and its Irish hierarchy unless otherwise noted.

9 Eamon de Valera had a number of disputes with the Catholic Church on subjects as diverse as: education and the country's relationship with Spain during the Spanish Civil War.

10 Speech by Lemass, Dublin, 25 June 1961 (NAI, S16947/5).

11 Quoted in Brian Farrell, *Seán Lemass* (Dublin, 1991), p. 72.

12 Quoted in J. H. Whyte, *Church and State in Modern Ireland, 1923–1970* (Dublin, 1971), p. 107.

13 Ibid.

14 *Irish Times*, 18 February 1966, quoted in Whyte, *Church and State*, p. 108.

15 Tom Garvin, *Preventing the Future: Why was Ireland so Poor for so Long?* (Dublin, 2004), pp. 71–2.

16 McQuaid to Rev. Ettore Felici, 15 April 1951 (DDA, McQuaid Papers, Govt Box 4, AB 8/B).

17 Noel Browne, *Against the Tide* (Dublin, 1986), p. 210.

18 Report from Archbishop McQuaid to the General Meeting of the Hierarchy, 14 October 1952 (DDA, McQuaid Papers, Govt Box 4 AB 8/B, p. 1.).

19 Ibid.

20 Ibid.

21 Ibid.

22 Ibid., pp 1–2.

23 McQuaid to Cardinal D'Alton, 8 September 1952 (ibid.).

24 Ibid.

25 The hierarchy was chiefly concerned with the possibility that adoption would facilitate the legal adoption of illegitimate Catholic children by Protestant families in Northern Ireland. See Mike Milotte, *Banished Babies: The Secret History of Ireland's Baby Export Business* (Dublin, 1997).

26 Whyte, *Church and State*, p. 276–7.

27 McQuaid to D'Alton, 8 September 1952 (DDA, McQuaid Papers, Govt box 4, AB 8/B).

28 Ryan to McQuaid, 10 September 1952 (ibid.).

29 Report from Archbishop McQuaid to the General Meeting of the Hierarchy, 14 October 1952, p. 9 (ibid.). The report was amended by McQuaid to provide a more comprehensive report for the papal nuncio, 7 November 1952; the following references are from the amended report. The meeting with Ryan took place at the Archbishop's House, 6 October 1952.

30 Ibid., pp 9–10.

31 Ibid., pp 10–11.

32 Ibid., p. 11.

33 Ibid., p. 12.

34 Ibid.

35 Ibid.

36 Ibid.

37 Ibid., p. 13.

38 *Irish Independent*, 6 November 1952.

39 McQuaid to Lemass, 6 November 1952 (DDA, McQuaid Papers, Govt Box 4, AB 8/B).

40 Ibid.

41 McQuaid to papal nuncio, 7 November 1952 (ibid.).

42 Ibid.

43 Ibid.

44 Quoted in John Horgan, *Seán Lemass: The Enigmatic Patriot* (Dublin, 1991), p. 151.

45 Ibid.

46 See Ruth Barrington, *Health, Medicine and Politics in Ireland, 1900–1970* (Dublin, 1987), pp 230–1.

47 Memorandum by McQuaid, 10 December 1952 (DDA, McQuaid Papers, Govt box 4 AB, 8/B).

48 Minutes of a meeting between Lemass, Ryan and the Episcopal Committee, 10 December 1952 (ibid.).

49 Ibid.

50 Ibid.

51 Ibid.

52 The letter is reproduced in Whyte, *Church and State in Modern Ireland*, Appendix C.

53 The *Irish Times* was not the archbishop's newspaper of choice. Its editors upset McQuaid when it published the correspondence with Noel Browne TD relating to the 1951 Mother-and-Child Scheme.

54 Archbishop Kinane of Cashel to de Valera, May 1953 (DDA, McQuaid Papers, Govt Box 1, AB 8/B).

55 Browne, *Against the Tide*, pp 218–19.

56 Ibid., p. 213.

57 See Barrington, *Health, Medicine and Politics*, p. 241; Browne, *Against the Tide*, p. 297; Dermot Keogh, *Twentieth Century Ireland: Nation and State* (Dublin, 1998), p. 79.

58 Quoted in Horgan, *Lemass*, p. 324.

59 Constitution of Ireland, 1937, quoted in Tom Inglis, *Moral Monopoly: The Rise and Fall of the Catholic Church in Modern Ireland* (Dublin, 1998), p. 79.

60 Whyte, *Church and State*, p. 347.

61 Ibid.

62 By the time the committee issued its Report I 1967 Lemass had retired as Taoiseach: in January 1969 he announced that he would not stand for re-election to the Dáil.

63 Whyte, *Church and State*, p. 348.

64 *Irish Times*, quoted in John A Murphy, *Ireland in the Twentieth Century* (Dublin, 1989) p. 133.

65 McQuaid to Ettore Felici, 15 April 1951 (DDA, McQuaid Papers, Govt Box 4 AB8/B).

66 Lemass, interview with Michael Mills, *Irish Press*, 23 January 1969.

67 Ibid.

Chapter 5: *Lemass and the Introduction of Irish Television*

1 See *Dáil Debates*, 12 October 1966.
2 John Reith was the first Director General at the BBC. He advocated the use of radio for developing educational and cultural programs and not simply as a source of entertainment.
3 See Robert J. Savage, *Irish Television: The Political and Social Origins* (Cork, 1996).
4 J. J. Lee, *Ireland 1912–1985: Politics and Society* (Cambridge, 1989), p 373.
5 Savage, *Irish Television*, pp 117–28.
6 NAI DC, TW 894, Letter from Lemass to Blaney, 25 July 1957.
7 Lemass to Blaney.
8 Ibid.
9 NAI DT S14996B, Cabinet Notes, 25 October 1957.
10 NAI DC, TW894.
11 Ibid.
12 Ibid.
13 Ibid., letter to Leon Ó Broin from the Department of Industry and Commerce, 12 December 1957. The author of this correspondence was most likely Lemass, although the letter in this file is an unsigned copy.
14 In November 1957 Neil Blaney was replaced as Minister by Seán Ormonde.
15 NAI DC TW 894, Memorandum from Seán Lemass to Seán Ormonde, Minister of Posts and Telegraphs, 17 December 1957.
16 NAI DC TW894, Memorandum from Ó Broin to Ormonde and Lemass.
17 Ibid., Memorandum from Lemass to Ormonde, 6 January 1958.
18 NAI DT S14996B, Draft proposal by Seán Lemass, 28 February 1958.
19 NAI DF S104/1/50, Memorandum from Moynihan Department of the Taoiseach to Ó Broin, 14 March 1958.
20 Leon Ó Broin, *Just Like Yesterday* (Dublin, 1985), p. 210.
21 Ibid., pp 209–10.
22 John Horgan, *Seán Lemass: The Enigmatic Patriot* (Dublin, 1997), p. 312.
23 NAI DT S14996D.
24 RTE, Minutes of the Television Authority 2 June 1960.
25 Ibid.
26 See Savage, *Irish Television*, for discussion on de Valera's speech made at the opening of the television service on New Year's Eve 1961.
27 NAI DT S14996D.
28 Ibid.

29 Ibid., According to John Irvine, a senior civil servant familiar with the 'policy directives', the speech that Lemass had been so obsessed with was never read out at the Television Authority's inaugural meeting. Instead, it appears to have been given by Lemass himself at a dinner celebrating the first meeting of the authority in 1960. Author's interview with John Irvine, 1990.

30 NAI DT S14996D.

31 Ibid.

32 Ibid.

Select Bibliography

Archives and libraries

Dublin Diocesan Archives
National Archives of Ireland
National Library of Ireland, Manuscripts Collection
Public Record Office, Belfast
Public Records Office, Kew, UK

Select Bibliography

Andrews, C. S., *Man of No Property* (Dublin, 2001).

Bew, Paul and Henry Patterson, *Seán Lemass and the Making of Modern Ireland* (Dublin, 1982).

Bloomfield, Ken, *Stormont in Crisis: A Memoir* (Belfast, 1994).

Brown, Terence, *Ireland, A Social and Cultural History, 1922 to the Present* (Ithaca, 1985).

Evans, Bryce, *Seán Lemass: Democratic Dictator* (Cork, 2011).

Fallon, Brian, *An Age of Innocence: Irish Culture 1930–1960* (Dublin, 1998).

Fanning, Ronan, *Independent Ireland* (Dublin, 1983).

Ferriter, Diarmaid, *The Transformation of Ireland, 1900–2000* (London, 2004).

Foster, R. F., *Luck and the Irish: A Brief History of Change from 1970* (Oxford, 2008).

———, *Modern Ireland 1600–1972* (New York, 1988).

Fuller, Louise, *Irish Catholicism since 1950: The Undoing of a Culture* (Dublin, 2002).

Garvin, Tom, *Preventing the Future: Why was Ireland so Poor for so Long?* (Dublin, 2004).

Girvin, Brian, *From Union to Union: Nationalism, Democracy and Religion in Ireland* (Dublin 2002).

Girvin, Brian and Gary Murphy, *Seán Lemass and the Making of Modern Ireland* (Dublin, 2006).

Horgan, John, *Seán Lemass: The Enigmatic Patriot* (Dublin, 1997).

Jackson, Alvin, *Ireland, 1798–1998* (Oxford, 1999).

Kenny, Mary, *Goodbye to Catholic Ireland* (London, 1997).

Keogh, Dermot, *Twentieth Century Ireland, Nation and State* (Dublin, 1994).

Lee, Joseph, *Ireland 1912–1985: Politics and Society* (Cambridge, 1989).

Mulholland, Marc, *Terence O'Neill (Life and Times New Series)* (Dublin, 2013).

———, *Northern Ireland at the Crossroads: Ulster Unionism in the O'Neill Years, 1960–9* (London, 2000).

Ó Broin, León, *Just Like Yesterday* (Dublin, 1985).

O'Neill, Terence, *Ulster at the Crossroads* (London, 1969).

Savage, Robert, *A Loss of Innocence? Television and Irish Society 1960–72* (Manchester, 2010).

———, *Irish Television: The Political and Social Origins* (Cork, 1996).

———, 'Introducing television in the age of Seán Lemass', in *The Lemass Era, Politics and Society in the Ireland of Seán Lemass*, eds, Brian Girvin and Gary Murphy (Dublin, 2005).

———, 'Constructing/deconstructing the image of Seán Lemass's Ireland', in *Ireland in the New Century: Politics, Culture and Identity*, ed., Robert J. Savage (Dublin, 2003).[repeated name ok – essay author & book editor??]

Whyte, J. H., Church *and State in Modern Ireland, 1923–1970* (Dublin, 1971).

Index